IS CUBA SOCIALIST?

IS CUBA SOCIALIST?

René Dumont
translated by Stanley Hochman

THE VIKING PRESS

NEW YORK

Originally published in French under the title
Cuba est-il Socialiste?
Copyright © 1970 Editions du Seuil
English translation Copyright © 1974 by André Deutsch Ltd

Published in 1974 by The Viking Press, Inc.
625 Madison Avenue, New York, N.Y. 10022
SBN 670-40192-7
Library of Congress catalog card number: 70-164991

Printed in Great Britain

Thought must never allow itself to become subservient to either a dogma, a party, a passion, an interest, a preconceived notion, or anything else, unless it be to the facts themselves; for thought to become subservient is for it to cease to be.

Henri Poincaré
Motto of the Free University of Brussels

Nazis and Stalinists [think] that it is unnecessary to ask men's advice before doing what is thought to be best for them.... Don't put confidence in the rich, the powerful, and the masters, because for them the truth is whatever they find useful; and what's useful to people in positions of privilege is not useful to all.

Claude Roy
Moi je

Contents

Contents

Preface

THIS is my second book about the attempt to construct socialism in Cuba. In my first, which appeared in France in May 1964,* I explained why I first went to visit Cuba, a country where a positive spirited revolution was searching for an original, basically humanist, socialist ethos. At the head of the revolution at the time were two most unusual people: Fidel Castro and Che Guevara. I went to study Cuba – in order to help the country – and to write about it in an initial study of underdevelopment, a work designed as a theoretical basis for solving Cuba's economic problems as quickly as possible.†

I found in Cuba the traces of a magnificent struggle, and a people caught up in the joy of liberation; but I also found great economic disorder. Because I underlined these difficulties at a time when many Cubans thought that political liberation would provide a solution to their many problems I was introduced to the Prime Minister, and on May 20, 1960 I had the privilege of a long talk with Castro. First he asked me why I criticized Cuban achievement so severely, whereas Jean-Paul Sartre had recently praised Cuban accomplishments in all areas, including those he knew little about. Castro listened to me attentively as we talked, mainly on the subjects of agricultural techniques, and the intensification and diversification of Cuba's agronomic basis.

I know that Castro read with care the report that I sent on to him in June 1960. He recalled me, as an expert, in August 1960 and saw me again at the end of the month. At that time we spoke more

* *Cuba, socialisme et développement*, Editions du Seuil. It has been translated into many languages, and in 1970 was even published in the United States by Grove Press.

† *Lands Alive*, Merlin Press, London, 1964. Monthly Review Press, New York, 1968.

briefly: he explained the "peoples' farms" project, which was to take shape in 1961, and I immediately expressed serious reservations about it. I was recalled to Cuba as an expert again in 1963, this time by Carlos Rafael Rodriguez, then the Director of the National Institute of Agrarian Reform (INRA) and in charge of the state agricultural sector.

My third report to INRA completed, I wrote the book mentioned at the beginning of this preface; in it, my critical views on the Cuban economy were once again dominant. An agronomist, by definition, is never satisfied; and an old militant socialist can legitimately be worried by certain political structures, notably those that continued to be called socialist in the Soviet Union even when Stalinism was rampant. I had written that study primarily for Cuba, but also with future South American revolutions in mind, so that I could help them more quickly overcome the economic difficulties that inevitably occur at the beginning of a revolution. (Were Brazil and Mexico, respectively ten and six times more populous than Cuba, to repeat similar errors and make the same faulty economic improvisations, the Soviet Union could not possibly bail them out to the same extent that it had done with Cuba.)

During our meeting on June 29, 1969 which began my fourth investigative sojourn (this time I came as Castro's personal guest), Castro told me that he had read my books *Terres vivantes* and *Sovkhoz, Kolkhoz ou le problématique communisme*, but he did not mention my book on Cuba, no doubt to avoid discussing it, for he had certainly read it in Spanish translation. Now I have written this second book with the same intention of "constructive criticism" as the first. Castro has often said that he doesn't want apologetics, and none of my studies has fallen into that category.

In the hasty notes that I sent him every day during July there slowly emerged, amidst the technical observations and bits of advice that dominated initially, certain economic criticisms that inevitably touched on political matters. I felt that between socialists, even if their philosophical conceptions were different, a frank expression of opinion was a necessity. The result was a dramatic discussion followed by an invitation to visit Cuba again. My primary reason for accepting this invitation to Cuba was once more to help Cuban agriculture as much as I could. The problems posed by its development are so many and so complex that I obviously could not supply an adequate response to all of them, and naturally therefore I often referred the Cubans to specialists.

[I feel myself obliged – I might even say driven – to supply constructive criticism; I must give my opinions without reserve or omission. Throughout the world current attempts to build social-ism are all incomplete and imperfect – inevitably, since experience is lacking. Some of these attempts made the mistake of claiming, as Stalinism did, that quasi-perfection has already been achieved. If they continue along this road, they will be unable to evolve or adapt themselves quickly enough to historical circumstances and to the rapidly changing productive forces – thus risking the kind of fearful failures of which we already have too many examples.] The countries in the socialist camp display only certain elements of socialism, the principal ones being collective ownership, a planned economy, and the priority of collective needs. This is not enough. Political power in these countries has not been transmitted to the working class but has been retained by a more or less restricted group of managers, "the new class", as Djilas calls them.

[The form of socialism that I am advocating strives for the development of all through the reduction of injustice. This also requires more liberty – even in industry, but especially in the press, to enable different opinions to be heard. This form of socialism will make progress only if we are able to learn from criticism, from the most varied sources. The enemy is at the gate, but the best way to resist him is to build a saner, more viable economy, adapted to men who are, generally speaking, imperfect,] as I myself am. And God knows I'm imperfect!

I reminded Fidel Castro that an old professor like me, from old Europe, *has* to deal with such an undertaking within the frame-work of his own pedagogic traditions. These oblige him to look everywhere, even in certain sectors of the opposition, for ways to understand a problem. The fact that I was able to contact these sectors shows a certain degree of liberty. In Cuba, I quickly learned its limits.

A chief of state should always remember two proverbs, the first of which is Roman: "*De minimis non curat praetor* – the leader is not concerned with trifles"! The second is English: "Power corrupts, absolute power corrupts absolutely." If Castro does not want to tarnish his historical image, if he would still affirm himself as an inspiring socialist leader, he must strive for originality and show greater concern with satisfying his people's aspirations. Like the rest of us, he is in need of improvement; to achieve it, Castro should listen more calmly not only to those who anger him – whether out of conviction or self-interest – but also to those whose conception of socialism differs from his own.

In the first two chapters of this book I will try to summarize the first two periods of Cuban socialism: the guerilla movement and the "rebellion," followed by the era of centralized and bureaucratic planning. Next I will outline what the fourth period, that of the construction of communism, might be expected to be like – especially given the *données* of Castro and Guevara. Coming back to earth, I will then make a more detailed study of the third period (1968–70) of hard reality. I will show the over-hasty cost of progress during that time, and also the retention of original features and traditions in Cuban "socialism" – which hopes soon to eliminate material incentives but still accords many privileges to its managing class. We shall then be able to ask ourselves if the militarization of Cuba's economy permits the flourishing of socialism.

I am sure that, after so short a stay in Cuba to examine problems so complex and so difficult, I will irritate many readers, but I also know that I had to follow my thoughts through to their conclusion. I am the more ready to accept criticism of this book in that I know I may have been incorrectly informed about certain things, or unable to judge the proportion of the population to which certain observations apply.

The first French edition of this book appeared in March 1970 and the second in August 1971. For this American and English edition I have made a number of corrections and brought a few points up to date. My only desire is that this book should bring about a better understanding of Cuba, and, especially, that there should not be a further deterioration of the relations between Cuba and the United States. The two countries have, of course, very different political approaches, but now that President Nixon has so judiciously decided on a normalization of relations with Peking there is no longer any reason to delay a normalization of the relations between Washington and Havana. It is in the interests of both parties. The most severe criticisms in this book on certain political aspects of both countries in no way keep me from very sincerely hoping for their *rapprochement* in the interest of world peace.

For the first time in history humanity is capable of destroying itself. A decrease in the tension between the United States and Cuba would permit both countries to evolve toward more liberalism more easily. It was in that hope that I wrote this study.

I want to thank all the Cuban friends who helped me in this work, and especially Major Fidel Castro, Carlos Rafael Rodriguez, Hermès Herrera, the interpreter Hector Rodriguez, Faustino Pérez, Majors Garcia and Curbelo, Selma Diaz, Captain Charandan, and many others, in whose interest it is best that I give no names. Among the French, I received help from MM. Amadieu, François, Garnier, Labrousse, Levacher, and especially Meunier and Maya Surduts. The manuscript was helpfully criticized by MM. Meunier, Gutelman, Joshua, Chominot, Mazoyer, Huguet, and Caty. I alone am responsible for its contents.

René Dumont

The Romantic Rebellion
Assumes Power 1959-61

1. A nationalist and humanist revolution

Batista's dictatorship in Cuba was so abominable that once the rebels had demonstrated that they were capable of overthrowing it they were able to achieve near unanimity against it. "Victory was only possible for us because we united Cubans of all classes and all sectors around a single, shared aspiration," said Fidel Castro in New York's Central Park on April 24, 1959. "The Cuban revolution [is] the purest and the most generous," he added. A few days earlier, during a press conference in New York, Castro had specified: "I have clearly and definitively said that we are not communists.... The gates are open to *private* investments that contribute to the development of industry in Cuba.... It is absolutely impossible for us to make progress if we don't come to an understanding with the United States."

The invitation was clear, the hand frankly offered, the gaze steady: "The United States can help us by dealing with us fairly in economic matters and treating us with understanding." It was Castro's prime interest then to gain understanding of his revolution, in order to be able to establish new economic relations with the United States that would

> facilitate the industrialization of the country and the implementation of agrarian reform so that unproductive land can begin to produce. Democracy that talks only of theoretical rights and forgets the needs of man is neither sincere nor true. Neither is the dictatorship of a man nor the dictatorship of a class, of groups, of castes, nor of an oligarchy; liberty with bread, without terror, that's humanism.

Castro's rebellion against the Batista dictatorship which had been supported by Yankee imperialism and had become hated in

Cuba carried the great majority of the country behind a young and generous minority of the intelligentsia on a triple quest for liberty, a better life, and national independence. Only the slogan *"patria o muerte"*, "our country or death", was to last; but for a long time it was accompanied by an alternative slogan: "liberty or death." The humanist coloring of this Cuban socialism attracted peasants, workers, part of the intelligentsia and the bourgeois middle classes – groups that would not initially have accepted a declared Marxist-Leninist revolution. The Popular Socialist (communist) Party, especially strong in the cities, did not believe in the rebellion's chances of success. Carlos Rafael Rodriguez, one of Cuba's leading communists, was among the first to join Castro's rebellion in the Sierra Maestra, but many of the city dwellers who belonged to his July 26th Movement were anti-communist. It was for this reason that the general strike called by the Movement for April 9, 1968 failed.

Saverio Tutino tells us that as early as 1941 Rodriguez had maintained in a study of Cuban social classes that "there was no true national bourgeoisie, especially in the flourishing sugar sector, and that the small working class was suffused with the petty bourgeois psychology of its rural and artisanat origins." Tutino adds that "when Fidel Castro evoked the necessity for replying to violence by violence, the objective conditions for revolution seemed lacking in Cuba. Nevertheless Castro brought them into being – proof that a man's personality can be an objective factor and make a given situation change qualitatively."* Seen from the outside, conditions in Cuba in 1953 and 1956 seemed less favorable to a revolution than those in Russia in 1917, when urban misery and the slaughter of badly armed soldiers had bred widespread discontent and facilitated the revolt. Can one place Castro's decisive spirit above Lenin's? Yes, for his determination under riskier conditions. But he would be the first to object to the position I have assigned him.

The July 26th Movement was organized first in Havana and Pinar del Rio provinces, in cells whose "leaders – students or white-collar workers, rarely manual workers – almost all came from the petty bourgeoisie. A bourgeois avant-garde for a popular base," says Tutino justly. Castro's plea after his unsuccessful attack on the Moncado army post (the date of which, July 26, 1953, gave the name to his movement) was based on the union of classes. Without this

---

* *L'Octobre cubain*, Paris, 1969, p. 152.

union the rebellion could not triumph, for it could not expect success if based solely on a small working class, with an even smaller number of socially aware and determined members. A purely working-class revolt would have attracted only few troops and would have rallied against it the entire bourgeoisie, which had a near monopoly on education; it would surely have failed.

By 1959, therefore, we saw the triumph of a national liberation movement that, under the direction of a small group of revolution-aries coming largely from the intelligentsia and galvanized by Castro, little by little united the great majority of the population against tyranny. If Castro had not insisted against all odds on what seemed like the impossible, the very movement itself would have been destroyed. The beginnings had been very hard. "Civilian in origin, our little group clung to the Sierra Maestra but was not integrated in it. We went from hut to hut, we ate only when we could pay, we were barely tolerated.... Life was extremely difficult", recalled Che Guevara in a speech to the cultural society *Nuestro Tiempo* on January 27, 1959.

The very success of the Cuban revolution may constitute a heavy handicap for eventual and future South American revolutions. The bourgeoisie fully understand the fate that awaits them should similar rebellions triumph. It is this that makes them hesitate, and it helps to explain the guerillas' lack of success in recent years from Venezuela to Guatemala, from Colombia to Peru – to say nothing of Che Guevara's ill-fated Bolivian expedition.* (This is what makes the case of Peru so interesting – it is the first real in-stance of opposition between the military and the oligarchy. The military government there has already shown itself more radical than the Christian Democrats were in Chile or Venezuela.)

2. The rebel army and the first agrarian reform

As early as 1953 Fidel's brother Raul Castro, who had been a mem-ber of the Young Communist League, had gone somewhat further in revolutionary theory than his brother. "It is a matter not of giving the land to the peasants but of distributing it so as to get

---

* Where even the different factions within the communist party were unable to agree among themselves or about their support for Che Guevara. Moreover, to count on a generalized revolt of the Indians (there are none in Cuba) is to forget that for them every Spanish-speaking white man is suspect – the whites have so often betrayed them.

maximum return," he said. "The government has to be over-thrown so that the revolution can begin." The overthrow of the dictatorship was therefore only a beginning, and the presence of Che, Commandante Ernesto Guevara, was soon to reinforce this sense of the event. The beginnings were timid, under the auspices of a sort of National Front; but the bourgeois government of January 1959 resigned after February 15 and Castro, who had not wanted to appear to profit from the rebellion, at the age of thirty-two took over the post of Prime Minister, a position he still holds.

After his speech on January 27, Che Guevara took up a position to the left of the July 26th Movement:

> It will be up to the organized peasant masses to carry out the agrarian reform by imposing the law forbidding latifundia.... The peasants who have conquered the right to liberty after the triumph of the revolution must lead a collective action to demand democratically that there be a departure from this principle [that all land expropriation be preceded by payment of indemnities]. Without this no total and true agrarian reform can be fully achieved.

Nevertheless, on May 17, 1959, Castro's first agrarian reform law was promulgated at La Plata, in the heart of the Sierra Maestra, by the bourgeois President Urrutia (who was to be overthrown less than two months later). The preamble of this law aimed at stimulat-ing the development of industry and encouraging private initiative. It proposed to facilitate the development of new crops for national industry, increased exportation, and the enlargement of the domestic market.

> 1·5 per cent of the landowners, with 2,236 farms, accounted for 3·6 million hectares, or 46 per cent of national land; 111,000 farms of less than 27 hectares each amounted to 2·3 million hectares; 70 per cent of the farms accounted for only 12 per cent of the nation's land (of these last 62,000 were less than 10 hectares).... On the large farms the land has been badly managed, the return on cultivated acreage is very low, overly large areas are given over to extensive cattle raising, while waste land is neglected.

> The large landed estates – extensive and uneconomical – should preferably be replaced by cooperative production – scientific

and intensive – which has the advantage of large-scale production.

There was thus no question, and I have elsewhere emphasized the wisdom of this position,* of giving "land to the one who works it," thereby multiplying the peasant *microfundia*, the second scourge of agriculture in Latin America.

The law prohibited estates of more than four hundred hectares,† but this is a relatively large area; the countries of eastern Europe in 1945-8 had limited holdings to twenty hectares (Bulgaria) and fifty-seven hectares (Hungary). Renters and share-croppers received free of cost the land they cultivated, up to a limit of twenty-seven hectares. This was *reformist law*, whose very liberal, generous terms concerning the extent of land permitted as well as the indemnities to be paid,‡ were quickly pointed out. Several initial divisions§ were made with the enthusiastic collaboration of a land-owner who had aided the rebellion. At this time a large majority of the Cuban population, including some of the bourgeoisie, was still Fidelist. The enthusiasm of the Cuban people was at its height; later, their disillusionment was to reach equivalent proportions. For, while it was reformist law, its application was put in the hands of the rebel army, which was revolutionary in spirit; the indemnities were never to be paid.

In August 1959 the counter-revolutionaries demonstrated and many were arrested. On September 25, at the United Nations, Raul Roa emphasized Cuba's independence in a general condemnation of the intervention of the United States in Guatemala, the USSR in Hungary, France in Algeria, and China in Tibet. "We do not accept being forced to choose between the communist solution and the capitalist solution. . . . Cuba is governed in the name of the people, by the people, and for the people."

On November 25 all the key ministry posts were in rebel hands- the army to Raul Roa, the national bank to Che Guevara. And

---

* In *Problèmes agraires, Reforme agraire, et Modernisation de l'agriculture au Mexique*, Paris, 1969.

† Cane and rice plantations and stock farms whose yields exceeded the national average by fifty per cent could retain 1,340 hectares.

‡ The law provided for indemnification, based on the October 10, 1958 sale value, in the form of twenty-year negotiable bonds bearing a maximum interest of 4·5 per cent.

§ The first domain to be expropriated was that of a family named Castro at Biran, in Oriente province, at the foot of the Pinares de Mayari.

throughout 1960 the pace of hard-line reform continued to accelerate. The opposition press disappeared; collaborators lost their property; and after Mikoyan's visit to Havana when the American oil refineries in Cuba refused to process the cheaper Soviet crude oil they were nationalized, a development that brought about the United States' termination of the quota under which Americans bought Cuban sugar at a preferential price. By the summer of 1960 all American property in Cuba had been seized; by autumn most Cuban companies, many of which were pro-American, were also nationalized.

The United States, in rejecting the outstretched hand, accelerated the "hardening" of Cuban socialism and, in a way, forced Cuba to increase its economic relations with the socialist camp and therefore to look to it for political support as well.

The United States could scarcely have accepted nationalization without indemnity, for this would have created a dangerous precedent. But their intransigence cost them dear, and showed itself once again in Peru and Chile. Those who were later to be caught in the quagmire of Vietnam had already in Cuba given proof of their lack of long-term political intelligence.* Thus was the Cuban revolution radicalized under the pressure of events and the stupidity and stubbornness of the United States.

On August 11, 1960, in a speech by Castro that I have not forgotten because it was rather freely inspired by a report that I had submitted to him after my visit to Cuba in May, he announced that the agrarian *reform* was over, because from now on there was going to be a true agrarian *revolution*. In other words, there would be no more expropriation indemnities.

The delegates of the National Institute of Agrarian Reform (INRA), responsible for a little bit of everything, nationalized all over the place, eager and happy to conquer various economic strongholds. But there was still – as I had seen in Santa Clara in May 1960 – no recognition of the difficulties involved in managing an economy that had fallen into their hands so rapidly. It was a task for which most of them, trained as they were in the humanities, law, and medicine, were badly prepared. Even Pedrito Betancourt, a professor of rural economy at the Agronomic Institute of Havana, was more at home with books and economic theory, and when he was placed in charge of production zone No. 4, PR 4, he made the worst sort of imprudent mistakes, clearing rocky land suitable for

* See Claude Julien, *L'Empire Americain*, Paris, 1968.

forestry in order to plant orchards, which in addition to everything else were far from any important market.*

From this time on, stringent criticism, even if of a technical nature, was no longer fashionable in the Cuban press. C. R. Rodriguez, who was well aware of the dangers in Cuba's immense economic disorder, introduced me to Fidel Castro on May 20, and I was invited to hold a press conference the next day during which I criticized a number of errors or inadequacies, but not a word of this criticism could be found in the next morning's papers. In spite of the importance that I was told Castro attached to my visits and my publications neither of them was ever mentioned in the Cuban press. Fidel considered me a "personal" expert more at his service than at Cuba's.

3. Che Guevara and the cooperatives

The estates confiscated in 1960 were given the name of cooperatives and baptized with the names of patriotic "rebels" who had died in combat. But they were cooperatives in name only. Their management was entrusted to INRA, which supplied all the credits, gave all the instructions, and got all the receipts. In reality, therefore, they were state farms. An elected management council was planned for them, but it was never intended to carry any weight with the administrator designated by INRA. The statutes governing the cooperatives were worked out behind closed doors and not in public discussions. It was planned that profits would first of all be used to pay for the beautiful new homes that were being built for some of the cooperatives' residents; the remainder was to be distributed in cash; no provision was made for investment.† However, these arrangements were never adopted. By August 1960, immediately after my second visit to Cuba, the cooperative formula was

* I noted the same error in 1963 on the island of Turriguano, and in 1969 to the east of Havana, where parts of intensively cultivated pastures were being established in an area covered with similar "dog's tooth" rocks. Socialism needs to dominate nature, but that is not the same as doing violence to it. In Spanish *Io te quiero* means both "I love you" and "I want you" – two very different sentiments.

† I had found these houses overly sumptuous and thought they contained too much imported merchandise. I was told, "Nothing's too fine for the people." "On the contrary," I replied, "what's too fine for them is what will cause their plates to be empty next year." That was in May 1960, and developments unfortunately proved that I was right.

definitively set aside, without those involved being either advised or consulted. They often told me, "We're determined to follow Fidel wherever he wants to lead us, but we'd like him at least to tell us where, and to be warned in advance." They weren't even asking to be consulted. These governmental decisions seemed to have been intended *for* the people, but it was not government *by* the people, who, it was assumed, didn't know what they needed – an attitude that is very different and leads to a situation in which it is forgotten that one is working for the people. Castro's speeches are a useful means of explaining the decisions of those in power, of educating, of inspiring, but they cannot be called real participation.

Just at that time, in mid-August 1960, Che Guevara received me at the headquarters of the National Bank at about ten o'clock one evening. I came straight to the point: "The workers on what you call cooperatives seem to me to have kept the mentality of paid employees. They used to have a capitalist boss and now they have another boss, the administrator, who represents the state. They have no sense of being on their own land, of being people who work for themselves. As I see it, they could best get this feeling at present from an agricultural production cooperative, where they could progressively develop a sense of collective co-ownership. That is a useful step in establishing devotion to the national interest. But the nation and the revolution are entities that are still too big, too abstract, to be really felt by most of the workers now."

Che Guevara reacted sharply. "We're not concerned with giving them a sense of collective co-ownership, group ownership. The problem is to develop their revolutionary awareness to the point of making them totally devoted to their revolution." Guevara often expressed this perpetual search for perfection, a search that was to lead him to despair. In 1962 he told the Young Communist League,

> The avant-garde attitude of the young people of the Playa Girón [Bay of Pigs, April 1961] . . . doesn't show up in their work. That seriousness which is essential to the undertaking of great tasks – and the greatest is the construction of a socialist society – is not reflected in their actual work. . . . Sometimes they skip work because they had a meeting, or because they went to bed late, or simply because they didn't feel like going to work, for no good reason.*

* Che Guevara, *Le socialisme et l'homme*, Paris, 1968.

Indeed it was true that Cuban workers, the descendants of sugar-plantation slaves or city-bred Gallegos, did not have the hard work traditions of European, Chinese, or North Vietnamese peasants. Castro often emphasized that pre-revolutionary work in the sun-drenched cane fields had been not only harsh and badly paid, but shadowed always by the threat of unemployment. However, this unemployment, when hunger didn't twist your guts, was also a time of leisure, a looked-for rest that sometimes took on the aspect of a holiday. Under Batista, the mental outlook of the unemployed and the *Lumpenproletariat* had been very different from that of Europe's peasants and workers.

Che Guevara tried to awaken the workers' pride and even their individuality: "We must accustom ourselves to think as a mass, to act according to the initiatives of the masses and of our great leaders ... to behave like individuals, concerned with our own actions, concerned to besmirch neither our own names nor that of the League."* When Che Guevara was gone, these nascent individuals were soon made into soldiers, and initiative was then openly and completely reserved to the leaders – as in fact it always had been.

4. Statist centralization; heretical revolution

On August 26, 1960 the Chilean Jacques Chonchol and I were received by Fidel Castro in his house at Cienaga de Zapata, where he was trying to develop tourism by an expensive plan for raising crocodiles. After listening to a rather brief report on my work, Castro explained his *granjas del peublo* (people's farms) project. This involved gigantic administrative, centralized undertakings; all expenditures paid out from the national budget and all receipts paid into it. Of course this meant that nobody, from the top administrators to the lowliest of the workers, would have any interest in seeing that the farms made a profit; you can be sure that they did not!

The *tiendas del pueblo* (people's stores) were supposed to bring the peasant consumer goods at the best prices. I had vainly suggested that a turnover tax be used to feed investment funds; but the need to increase such funds had not yet been recognized. Salaries rose quickly; imports were drastically reduced because of the lack of

---

* Che Guevara also remarked upon the inadequacy of the latter: "The Young Communist League has been rather lacking in creative spirit. It has been too docile, too respectful, too little disposed to set itself problems." Was his spirit of protest always acceptable? When it no longer was, could he stay on?

convertible currency; scarcity of goods soon followed, beginning early in 1961 and becoming more and more serious in 1962. The lowering of rents further augmented buying power, and production could not keep up with it. It was forgotten that one could not distribute more commodities than were available; soon the distribution itself became wasteful. The idea had been to make Cuba an attractive showcase for the revolution the government hoped was near in other Latin American countries (the situation had its analogue in revolutionary Russia), but here was Cuba driven to make, not only "revolution in one country" (aid from the socialist camp was soon forthcoming), but also what was for a long time the only revolution in Latin America.

This revolution showed itself to be "heretical" on a number of points. In Havana in February 1960 Mikoyan had had the wisdom to acknowledge that "Cuba proves that reality is more complex than theory." Called into life by an intelligentsia that got more help from the peasants than from the working class, this revolution tried to raise the living standards of the rural inhabitants immediately, whereas in the Soviet Union this goal was for a long time sacrificed to the needs of industrialization. More radical from the beginning, the Cuban revolution rightly rejected the idea of dividing up the latifundia; but it also rejected the idea of producers' cooperatives. The years that followed were in no way to confirm the wisdom of this precipitation. Nobody can say, *a posteriori*, what would have resulted from opting for a cooperative solution – it would unquestionably have met with great difficulties – but I continue to think that those difficulties would not have been as great as those actually encountered, for economic errors would have immediately affected the earnings of the cooperators and solutions would have been more urgently sought.*

After the Bay of Pigs attack Castro officially proclaimed a socialist revolution that was already realized in fact. On April 15, 1961 he once again spoke of "the socialist and democratic revolution of the common man, by the common man, and for the common man" – a formula inspired by the great "republic" to Cuba's north.

---

* I have been told that the latifundia workers didn't share the peasant mentality. But there are also peasants in Cuba, and cooperatives could have been set up with them that would have provided healthy competition for the state farms. (In 1961–2 there were plenty of sugar cane cooperatives in competition with the *granjas*, but the latter received heavy advantages and one cannot really judge the competition fairly.)

2

Centralized Planning and Bureaucracy 1961-8

1. Unifying the revolution

As we have seen, Castro's group – supported by the revolutionary wing of the July 26th Movement and its ally, the Popular Socialist Party – took over all political power during 1959, successively eliminating various bourgeois factions. Beginning in 1960, partly in reaction against the unacceptable pretensions of the United States, it hastened agrarian reform, nationalized the principal sectors of industry and commerce, and thereby conquered *economic* power in a *de facto* socialization. In 1961 Castro officially announced himself a socialist, and the various revolutionary movements were organized into a single group.

The United Revolutionary Organizations (ORI) united the Fidelistas of July 26th, the Communist (formerly Popular Socialist) Party, and the members of the March 13th Directory, which mainly represented an urban resistance force, notably those who had attacked the presidential palace on March 13, 1957. The middle classes left the country more and more rapidly. Cuba thus lost forty per cent of its doctors, including most of its medical school professors, as well as a large number of its agronomists, veterinarians, industrial engineers, and other immediately useful cadres.

A psychological attitude comparable to that of the Chinese revolutionaries during a somewhat analogous period (1949–51) would have enabled Cuba to retain more of these cadres. This would have required showing them, as Che Guevara had done, that technical competence and professional conscientiousness were still highly appreciated. But those who remained often found themselves placed under the orders of incompetent or mediocre, and sometimes arrogantly ignorant men. Their under-utilization, together with the contempt often shown them, led many into opposition who had only wanted a chance to serve.

Nor was the political handling of the peasants entirely skilful. One of the three rebel Escambray columns had not been able – as Castro had in the Sierra – to lead, reassure, and win them over. Many well-to-do peasants there, better off than those in the Sierra, bitterly resented the militia men "who had taken their cows without paying for them." The state wanted to buy all kinds of products quickly at prices of which the overall level seemed initially satisfactory (the situation is not comparable to the *de facto* spoilations of wartime communism in the Soviet Union) but the relations between prices were often ill-established, and the prices were quickly found to be lower than those on the free market which had sprung up as a result of scarcity. Moreover, "the base cadres sent by the revolutionary leaders [into Escambray] had almost all been trained in union work, and they often behaved like narrow-minded functionaries."* Considerable counter-revolutionary resistance groups formed in Escambray, and one entire peasant group was transplanted, or deported, under extremely difficult circumstances to Ciudad Sandino, west of Pinar del Rio province. There was also fighting at Matanzas and southeast of Havana in the Guines region.

Eventually, at the end of 1961, an attempt was made to establish a true political party, the United Party of the Socialist Revolution (PURS). Tutino has shown how two different political conceptions clashed in this effort – conceptions that nevertheless both called themselves Marxist-Leninist, this time without the least ambiguity. Castro wanted to recruit members by elections in which exemplary workers would be chosen; he wanted "a limited party, which would exclude opportunists in search of privileges." If only he had succeeded!

On the other hand, Anibal Escalante, a veteran communist who was in charge of party organization, wanted a membership with "a minimum of ideological preparation. On this basis he began to discredit the true artisans of the revolution and to gloss over the hesitations of last-minute revolutionaries . . . who monopolized responsibilities, and thrust aside others because of their low level of political training."

Fidel Castro responded to this challenge in a speech on March 13, 1962, the fifth anniversary of the attack against Batista's presidential palace. Then, on March 26, he denounced the Escalante group's

---

* Tutino, *L'Octobre cubain*, p. 238.

attempts to control the party, the government, and the administration. This decision probably saved Cuba from an early neo-Stalinist phase, which could have been extremely pernicious.

> When errors are not submitted to self-criticism, enemies profit [Castro said]. Sectarianism is the fundamental error. . . . Escalante has converted the party apparatus into a nest of privileges, tolerances, and favors of all kinds. His inner group has nominated, revoked, ordered, governed . . . a party of servants, of snobs, and of proud men. . . . An army of drilled and domesticated revolutionaries. . . . [They lack] honor, honesty, uprightness, and absence of passion and personalism with which revolutionary leaders must speak.

Castro might well read now what he said then; it has lost nothing of its relevancy. If only he would heed his own words!

2. Literacy

The year 1961 was the Year of Literacy, a magnificent campaign during the course of which tens of thousands of students, who were then real volunteers, went to the most remote villages, the most isolated mountain areas, to teach illiterate peasants how to read and write. It was also a political education campaign that increased receptivity to the revolution among the peasantry, the more so since it was soon followed by the construction of rural schools and clinics. (Counter-revolutionary resistance groups furnished this movement with its martyr when twenty of them got together to lynch a sixteen-year-old high-school student as punishment for his devotion to it.)

Some people, myself included, regretted that the peasants were taught F as in Fidel or fusillade and not P as in plow, and that the campaign was not, despite some efforts, adequately followed through to basic professional training. Those who had been taught to read were later offered evening classes, and some have now obtained an elementary school diploma by means of these night schools. But it requires quite a bit of courage to attend these classes. They are given late in the evening, partly because of the bourgeois origins of the teachers, who are not particularly concerned with their students missing their sleep, and who disregard the fact that railway workers have to be on the job at six in the morning and that buses are rare at midnight.

3. Over-centralization in the economy

"Planified management of an economy is the result of the nationalized character of its industries. . . . Since 1961 Czech experts have supplied Cuba's central planning staff with techniques and norms that are ill-suited to Cuba – whose economy was underdeveloped, unbalanced, dependent, disjointed – [and offered these] completely devoid of statistics."*

Given the circumstances, I had urged Castro as early as 1960 to begin with rather small, autonomous agricultural production co-operatives. The cooperatives could have been directed by the former managers of the expropriated lands, who had practical experience, until such time as new young technicians were trained. Financial autonomy would have made it possible to encourage the efficiency of the workers, for their earnings would have been directly linked to their productivity. This would have facilitated the maintenance of a land rent paid to the state. (This basic idea is dangerously ignored in socialist countries, even though it is part of the 1848 Communist Manifesto. I have tried to point out its usefulness even in the USSR.)

Such an approach would have required giving the remaining peasants a certain amount of freedom in marketing their crops and in setting up local markets for perishable products. The extremely high scarcity prices in 1961 could have encouraged increased production and, hence, lower prices. In September 1963 the Russian economist Bondarchuk explained to my Cuban colleagues that in the Soviet Union sixty per cent of the distribution of perishable products was then accounted for in the free or cooperative sector, state-controlled commerce accounting for only forty per cent. This discreet observation received no more attention than had my less discreet advice.

The cooperative formula was, then, rejected from the beginning, for the revolutionary leaders were eager to hasten the job by "stratifying" (which is not the same thing as socializing) almost all the economy. At the same time they wanted to win wage-earners over to their cause by means of wage increases and improved working conditions, so that between 1959 and 1961 salaries increased by about sixty per cent, whereas agricultural production increased by perhaps only ten per cent in 1959–60. Bondarchuk told me in 1963

---

* Michel Gutelman, *L'Agriculture socialisée à Cuba*, Paris, 1967, p. 72.

that each time a worker produced a peso of wealth, he received two pesos in salary!

A very rough study had led me to conclude that from 1958 to 1963 the productivity of an agricultural work day had decreased by about one half.* In 1963 the harvests were probably only seventy-five per cent of those in 1960, whereas the number of work days had been rising rapidly. Though unemployment had disappeared, production had not benefited. This was obvious proof that the Cubans' average revolutionary awareness was not at the level that a structure so "stratified" would require. One had only to watch two crews at work – one paid by the day and noticeably casual, and the other paid by the job and very active – to understand that the workers were still responsive to material incentives, although already there was talk of abandoning them. As it happened, rationing quickly reduced the value of money; and beginning in 1962 Che Guevara denounced absenteeism (without much result it would seem). This absenteeism, however, has never been checked and in its own way perpetuates a kind of unemployment.

The situation had become almost catastrophic by 1963. An effort had been made to end Cuba's dependence on a single crop, sugar. But though the diversification of crops is necessary on a *national* level, we will see that it can easily be accompanied by *regional* specialization. The national leadership of INRA was unable to manage anything correctly. The *granjas del peublo*, soon to be called state farms, received successive and contradictory orders from various offices. Gutelman tells us that the 1963 production plan for Las Villas province did not get to the *granjas* until November. Some areas were never sown at all in 1963, after being plowed four times for four different crops.

Each *granja* had too much land, in too many unregrouped plots. Each produced from twenty to thirty-five different crops, often very badly. The culture of cotton, kenaf (fiber), peanuts, sunflowers, and most fruits and vegetables had been more or less unknown to both the workers and the technicians, who were usually familiar with

---

* A similar decline was even more pronounced on self-managed Algerian farms in 1962-8. The use of more labor – principally people who were previously unemployed – does not automatically bring about a rise in production. Production increases were obtained in China and North Vietnam, but not always in proportion to the increased number of man hours. When only the work factor is increased, in the virtual absence of tools, fertilizers and new techniques, beyond a certain point efficiency decreases.

sugarcane and sometimes a little stock farming, but the monthly INRA publication was concerned with propaganda rather than instruction. I vainly called for popular training pamphlets. (I finally saw some in 1969, but only for the use of managers and only for the very important crops; the effort still remains inadequate.) Since sugarcane had been held responsible for all the nation's ills, sugar production fell to 3·8 million tons in 1963, as against six million in 1961.

The sudden disappearance of Cuba from the world sugar market provoked a spectacular price rise: for several weeks sugar was up to thirteen cents a pound as against two cents a few months earlier. Beginning in early 1964 long-term delivery contracts were negotiated with the socialist countries at prices apparently as good as those that the United States had given Cuba: six cents a pound for the Soviet Union and China, 5·5 cents for Czechoslovakia and Poland (more cautious because of their own beet sugar production).

With these guarantees in hand, Castro swore upon the honor of his people (although it was *he* who undertook the obligation) to reach an annual production of ten million tons by 1970. Since the socialist countries had contracted for six million tons, Fidel's promise constituted a publicly announced challenge to the entire South American sugar economy. For Cuba, assured of selling most of its production at a good price, could look forward to "unloading" the rest. Yet when a Cuban agronomist, an important technocrat working for the Prime Minister, told me in 1969 that Cuba could produce sugar at one cent a pound, he was demonstrating a total lack of economic knowledge – one that was spreading dangerously without sufficient corrective action being taken by the big boss. In point of fact, it would appear difficult to go below an average of three or four cents a pound.

It was of course reasonable to return to a primary emphasis on the agricultural economy, but that may not have required the abandonment of so many industrial projects. Che Guevara may have been right in wanting to encourage industry, notwithstanding some of his errors. It seemed equally necessary to re-establish the sugar priority, since both the natural and historic conditions for sugar were so favorable in Cuba, but was it necessary during this initial phase to surpass the economically feasible 8·5 annual tons that Che Guevara had proposed at the Punta del Este conference in the autumn of 1961? Probably not. It would no doubt have been more economical to emphasize other exports, especially early winter vegetables and mining products (nickel, chrome and cobalt – later, iron and copper). And the total abandonment of cotton is no more justifiable than was the excessive craze the Cuban government originally developed for this plant; dozens of Soviet cotton-picking machines are now rusting in sheds. Two factories for processing kenaf also remain very under-utilized.

In addition the country's pre-revolutionary American-made equipment, as well as the inadequacy of certain industries in socialist countries, obliged Cuba to buy a significant amount of goods from the west, and therefore to procure convertible currency. For years Cuba vainly asked the Soviet Union to pay for a part of its sugar purchases in dollars, but the very announcement of this policy of "international class struggle" in the interests of sugar dumping accelerated the decline of the sugar market, once the quotas formerly "granted" by the United States had been filled by Cuba's new socialist clients. This decline may have contributed to the revolts in Santo Domingo, where marines quickly re-established the only type of order acceptable to Washington, and to the closing of some archaic Argentine sugar refineries in Tucuman, where a tough military government succeeded the pseudo-democrats. None of this can be said to be propitious to future South American revolutions.

4. The second agrarian reform and the reorganization of the granjas

On October 2, 1963 a decree issued during the night and enforced at dawn everywhere in Cuba expropriated all landed property of between sixty-seven and four hundred hectares. This spelled the virtual elimination of all middle and large farmers, many of whom in any case had lost confidence in the government and some of whom had even actively aided the counter-revolutionaries. But some of these farmers had definite technical skills, and were at the same time more productive and less parasitical than the latifundia owners; they could have been salvaged, especially as estate managers. Indeed they could have managed their own farms, since they knew them well and the INRA of the period seemed unable to take on the increased work load.

But it was at this moment that some interesting studies made at the Institute of Physical Planning were applied on a larger scale. The incorporation of lands resulting from this second agricultural reform, and the unification of the three different types of people's farms with their three separate commands into a single organization of state farms, progressively eliminated a certain number of errors, beginning with the largest which was the chasm that separated the decision-makers from the farms themselves. The *granjas* of a single region were now federated into groups, the *agrupaciones*, so that the command centers tended to become better informed.

Some book-keeping autonomy – which was still far from real management autonomy – was established at the *agrupacion* level; newly trained book-keepers began to straighten out the previously muddled accounts. Until 1966 the *agrupacion* received funds via the plan* to meet its foreseeable expenses; allocations were a bit more in line with real possibilities. After 1966 the *agrupacion* received all its supplies directly, without these being charged to its account; and a small fund was made available to pay wages. The all too frequent delays in the delivery of fertilizers, pesticides, spare parts, etc., were now somewhat reduced (without, alas, disappearing; they still sometimes endanger an entire harvest). The excessive diversification of crops was progressively cut down as specialized *granjas* were created, responsibilities were more clearly defined at each level, and unity of direction was firmly established. "Such rigidity in the idea of a unified authority seems," Gutelman wrote, "as the example of other socialist countries shows, to bring in its wake considerable delays in decision-making. These delays stem from the physical inability of the decision-makers to absorb the information they receive quickly enough." As we shall see (in 1969) decisions were often made without the information being digested at all, and the results were costly!

To sum up, attempts were made from 1963 to 1968 to correct error by successive adjustments but without solving the fundamental problems of self-management or of material work incentives. Work norms were established, and these encouraged the most dedicated workers, but absenteeism continued: when a worker had earned enough money during the first third of the month to pay for his personal and family rations, he was no longer interested in working to accumulate useless cash, since black market prices had increased beyond his reach.

* See page 33.

5. Provincial food autonomy, special plans, and overall bureaucracy

The dispersion over the entire countryside of products needed in Cuba's industrial transformation made the rational localization of factories impossible and pointlessly increased the distance over which material had to be transported. The *granjas* were reluctant to undertake new kinds of crops which would require better trained cadres. Havana, an outpost of the economy's tertiary sector, had been as close economically to the United States as to the rest of Cuba and somewhat parasitically drew on all the provinces for its needs. Most bananas, for example, came from Oriente province and had to be transported six hundred miles to the market places of the capital. Losses en route increased because nobody was interested in keeping them down.

What followed, under the direct inspiration of Fidel Castro and under the control of his technical teams, was a series of special plans for agricultural and stock farming. Given priority over all other production, these plans were able to requisition all the men and means they required – which of course endangered the work and the supplying of the regular units, the *granjas*. In 1960 I had suggested that the hypertrophied city of Havana be surrounded with a "green belt" of market-gardens and fruit farms as far as the adaptability of the land and the availability of water allowed. I urged that a second concentric belt for the production of "*viandas*" (taros, sweet potatoes, potatoes, plantains, etc.) and dairy farming should be established. Other cities could have adopted the same plan on a suitable scale. I had even suggested a plan by which each major agricultural production unit could supply itself with a significant portion of its own food supply. The prolongation and aggravation of scarcities only emphasized the value of this project, which was never undertaken.

In any case during 1967-8 there was a slow development – under the pressure of increasing transport difficulties – of the principle of alimentary autonomy for each province. Vertical integration of principal agricultural products under the control of the processing factories had already developed. The Tobacco Board, for example, took care of growing, harvesting, preparing, and selling tobacco, including everything from seed bed planting to exporting cigars. (After 1969 cultivation was removed from the board's control.) It had to overcome a heavy quality handicap – quality fell off sharply

2

after the rigid imposition of uniform prices – for a crop that in 1969 was still about ninety per cent in the hands of peasants. The national Poultry Board established large egg-producing units that seemed reasonably efficient, but the mortality rate was still high. Eggs were unrationed only for a brief time, and chicken is still scarce.

Meanwhile INRA was trying to manage its *granjas* and straighten out the big 1963 mess. It was the time of organization tables by which each administration tried to justify its inflated number of employees by Parkinson's Law (which also operates in socialist governments that have not experienced a cultural revolution). Although more or less ill-informed, the central bureaucracy nevertheless still tried to manage everything. Their skill in multiplying useless quantities of paper notwithstanding, the armies of office employees did scarcely any work – with some honorable exceptions, notably the Ministries of Industry and Foreign Trade, the Institute of Physical Planning, and the army.

During this time the rural exodus continued at an accelerated pace. Every peasant's son, even if very little educated, wanted to work in the city. It seemed much easier and a lot better paid than cutting sugarcane in the sun. The number of children in school instead of in the fields rose sharply – a sure guarantee of a better future for the country. But this development should have been anticipated. As it was, it only angered the cane-cutters, who had to delegate some of their manpower for essential office business, even if it was only a matter of procuring work gloves. Still, all in all, the *machetero*'s level of revolutionary consciousness, despite the deficiencies that I have pointed out, was generally far above that of the bureaucratized petty bourgeois.

The need for an anti-bureaucratic struggle slowly became evident, but the form of the struggle was to remain ill-defined. Castro began to fulminate against the makers of organization charts. Only a degree of decentralization could help the situation and on paper it appeared to be in progress. But "the fact that a plan is established at the base is not in itself a guarantee of non-bureaucratism. The *real participation* of workers in planning has to be *really* organized." With some exceptions – Che Guevara was one – there was less and less talk of participation. In actuality Cuban society remained authoritarian and hierarchized; Fidel maneuvered it as he saw fit. The result was a sort of militaristic society; but let us not jump ahead of our story. . . .

6. The peasants and the cooperatives

After the first agrarian reform peasants with less than sixty-seven hectares had been grouped into the National Association of Small Peasants (ANAP), which organized them politically and was supposed to help them with advice, credit facilities, the few available tractor services, etc. All this was done on a very limited scale. Gutelman estimates that the fifteen million pesos in investment credits received annually by these peasants merely "financed the maintenance of existing capacities". Until 1967 this sector of the Cuban economy remained all but wholly neglected – and virtually unorganized: here again Cuba's agrarian politics were unusual.

No attempt at enforced collectivization was made; though the Party had not forbidden the peasants to organize small production cooperatives, it never really favored them. Castro decided that peasants who wanted to band together in cooperatives should first be denied this method; their demands were to be met only if the peasants insisted. The 270 agricultural and stock farming cooperatives, accounting for 20,000 hectares in 1966, were therefore mostly family groupings, and their number did not increase in the future; by 1969 officials had made their lack of sympathy for them evident. The cooperatives were, in fact, considered part of the private sector and were progressively incorporated into the state plans after 1969. Here too "stratification" was preferred to cooperation, and the issue of whether this respected the wishes of the peasants was never posed: their harvests were arbitrarily accepted or refused, and in addition were not well paid for.

During most of the 1960s – most particularly during the difficult period of 1961-7 – responsibility for the failure of the Cuban economy was often, and justifiably, laid at the door of underdevelopment, lack of cadres, meager training. But this explanation seems inadequate to me. Decisions made by the small group of Cuba's leaders had deliberately created *statist* production structures that would have required a level of revolutionary consciousness far superior to what could be seen in Cuba. But nothing in Cuba yet indicates that a change of orientation is on the way. At the end of 1971 no trace of an NEP can be seen on the horizon. Even talk of it arouses indignation and is quickly followed by references to "the Yugoslavian heresy, the peaceful return to capitalism."

7. Che Guevara's hoped-for "perfect" society

"In our system we focus on the future, on accelerated development of consciousness and, by means of consciousness, of productive forces," wrote Che Guevara in the June 1964 issue of *Cuba Socialista* in response to an article by Charles Bettelheim that had appeared in the same magazine two months earlier. "At a given moment the revolutionary forces take power, move full speed ahead, decree the socialist character of the revolution, and undertake the construction of socialism. The avant-garde, in its awareness, can foresee an entire series of steps to be achieved and to force the march of events . . . within the limits of what is objectively possible."

This was the same Che Guevara who had spoken so sharply of the weaknesses and inadequacies of Cuba's young workers and their organizations. This pure idealist somehow wanted to force the hand of destiny; he was to encounter more and more obstacles. After epic discussions with Carlos Rafael Rodriguez, and no doubt with Castro himself, especially in 1964–5, he was better able to judge the enormous difficulties involved in realizing his dream of a "perfect" society – particularly in the Cuban milieu, but everywhere else as well.

His last important study, *Man and Socialism in Cuba*, has since become a kind of ideological testament.

> One of our fundamental ideological tasks is to find the way to perpetuate heroic attitudes in everyday life. . . . The initiative comes from Fidel or the high command of the revolution: it is explained to the people, who make it their own. . . . But, at times the state makes mistakes. . . . The mechanism is obviously not sufficient to ensure a sequence of efficacious measures; what is missing is a more structural relationship with the masses. . . . To build communism, it is necessary to change man at the same time as one changes the economic base.

To change man: this brings us to the heart of the problem of socialism, if not of the future of humanity.

> The avant-garde is ideologically more advanced than the masses; the latter is acquainted with the new values, but not well enough. While in the former a qualitative change takes place which permits them to make sacrifices as a function of their vanguard character, the latter are less conscious and must be subjected to

pressure . . . this is the dictatorship of the proletariat being exercised not only upon the defeated class but also individually *upon the victorious class.* . . . We are not yet at the point where the institutions of the revolution can be achieved. We are seeking a *perfect* identification between the government and the community as a whole. . . . Scholasticism has held back the development of Marxist philosophy. . . . We must agree that we are still in the cradle. . . . Socialism is young and makes mistakes.*

8. Che Guevara departs

In 1965 Castro proclaimed that it was better to have a revolutionary with no technical competence than someone with technical competence who was not revolutionary. This was a decision of the highest importance. Che Guevara had often said the contrary because he knew that he could control technical competence more easily than the degree of revolutionary spirit. During the mid-1960s there was another increase in the exodus of technicians, who were replaced in positions of responsibility by revolutionary conformists; these latter did not actually do the work so much as *seem* to do it – and above all they approved of everything. Che Guevara wouldn't – indeed couldn't – admit the failure of the new man, but he now believed that his specific task as Minister of Industry was more and more difficult to reconcile with his search for perfection. "When our factories are directed from Havana by cablegram and telephone, they should operate like perfect clockwork," he remarked. But there was sand in the works.

Che Guevara left on a grand tour that took him overseas from November 1964 to March 14, 1965, primarily to the socialist and underdeveloped countries. He wrote to his mother that he was going to spend a month cutting cane before devoting five years to directing a factory under his former ministry. (He had evidently discreetly resigned as minister.) His mother, "an old lady who would like the whole world to convert to socialism," reproached him for his attitude. But the decision had been made. Given the difficulty of his task, which he had finally to admit could not lead to perfection, given the growing compromises in Cuban politics, he thought he could be more useful to the cause of world revolution as a guerilla. He was not unaware of the risks: "I am one of those adventurers

* *Socialism and Man in Cuba*, Stage I, London, 1968.

who risk their lives to prove that what they believe is true."* Che Guevara was a pure soul who was to end as a martyr, assassinated by fascists, but also abandoned by most of the Bolivian communists (who, he irritably wrote in his diary, were "pigs"). For the young his death lit up the luminous path toward revolution, whose difficulties they do not see.

Che Guevara's idealism forced universal respect, even among some of his enemies. But respect does not mean unconditional acceptance of all of his ideas. In the final analysis he was looking for a transition toward communism. In examining this issue, I should like therefore to skip over the third period of Cuban socialism (1968–71) for the moment and try to examine how Castro and the other Cuban leaders saw the fourth period of Cuban socialism, which was in principle to lead the country to a communist society.

---

* Gonzalez and Sanchez Salazar, *Che Guevara en Bolivie*, Paris, 1969.

3

Sketches of the March toward Communism

1. The parallel construction of socialism and communism

Marx warned us that it was dangerous to fix the features of a communist society too precisely in advance, that it was better to take a pragmatic approach. On May 1, 1966 Castro had thus modestly classified himself as an "apprentice revolutionary."

> We must not ignore experience, but we must also guard against a mechanical copying of [foreign] formulas.... Communism can be constructed in a single country....* Communism and socialism must be built in parallel. In aiming for socialist goals we must neither mortgage nor renounce the development and formation of communist man....
>
> It will be possible to establish communism in human society only when egoism disappears. Abundance can be achieved without communism. Communism will be abundance without egoism.... When we have achieved satisfactory levels of nourishment, education, medical care and housing we will not think it our duty to strive so that each one of us may have his own automobile before concerning ourselves about whether or not each family in those countries which are behind us owns at least a plow.†

At the same time, in order to obtain that abundance more quickly, Castro asked that a million Cuban women be incorporated into

---

* Disputable. The encirclement of a country going it alone on a path reviled by its neighbors would make necessary a strong state, a police, an army, and an ever-growing bureaucracy. However, one can conceive of an evolved, rich, and humane socialist civilization developing the fraternal sense.

† This lesson in international solidarity was indirectly addressed to the USSR, with whom relations were not of the best at that time. It displeased the USSR to see Cuba's commercial deficit swell too quickly, especially since that country had refused to fall into line politically.

production by 1976; this in a country where they were happy to stay
at home, as their protective husbands preferred. He also praised
"voluntary" work: the communist child was to learn to love both
study and work; by the time he was six he was to cultivate a lettuce
patch. More and more schools were to be built in the midst of the
fields, where the pupils were expected to join in the work. They had
to "learn that work was not degrading, was not a sacrifice but a
pleasure, a most happy and most agreeable thing, no longer a duty
but a moral necessity."

On the fifteenth anniversary of the Moncada attack, in 1968, Fidel
returned to the theme that "the great task of the revolution is to
form the new man Che spoke of, the man whose conscience is truly
revolutionary, truly socialist, truly communist":

> We don't pretend to be the most perfect revolutionaries, but we
> have our way of interpreting socialism, Marxism-Leninism,
> communism. . . . No human society has attained to communism
> . . . in which man will be able to achieve the degree of under-
> standing and fraternity that he has sometimes reached within the
> narrow framework of the family. . . .

> We aspire to a mode of life in which man will not need money to
> satisfy his basic needs for food, clothing, and entertainment.
> This is already the case with medical care and education. . . . The
> revolution wants to equalize incomes from the bottom up by
> raising the incomes of those who earn less. . . . Is the engineer's
> income going to be reduced? No, but one day the *machetero* –
> actually, there will no longer be any, so let's say the truck driver –
> will earn what the engineer earns. For who has paid for the latter's
> studies? The people. . . . Our task is not to create a conscience by
> means of wealth, but to create wealth by means of conscience. . . .
> We have to develop conscience to the same extent that we develop
> productive forces.

I wouldn't want to have to teach "revolutionary awareness" at the
University of Havana. This awareness is the heart of the problem,
and Castro knows it. "If man is incorrigible, only capable of progressing when motivated by egoism, incapable of developing his
conscience, then the learned economists are right, the revolution is
heading for catastrophe. . . . The struggle to achieve a superior form
of social life is one of the most difficult there is, one of the most
difficult paths on which a people can embark."

2. The promise of agricultural abundance

In all his speeches after late 1968 Fidel Castro promised extraordinary agricultural abundance, which he proposed to bring about
in a very short time. He predicted a *"quadrupling* of the country's
dairy production in two years, by the end of 1970," an unattainable
goal in the best of circumstances. In early 1969 he announced agricultural increases of fifteen per cent annually for the next twelve
years. (Later he specified that "production is to be doubled in the
next four years.") Fifteen per cent annually, compounded, means
quadrupling in ten years and, according to this hypothesis, another
doubling in the following six years. In twelve years Cuban agricultural production was therefore to be multiplied by 5·35!

This is a dizzying perspective for those who are aware that to date
the maximum rate of agricultural increase in a large country,
achieved by Mexico between 1946 and 1955, was recorded at eight
per cent. Even this eight per cent seems debatable to those who have
studied the situation more closely and who believe that the earlier
harvests were underestimated. (The example of Israel, with a nine
per cent annual increase over twenty years, hardly applies to Cuba.
Israel's was a quasi-colonial situation, with massive investments
largely financed from the outside, with a rapid influx of a population
that was on the whole very well educated, with a national awareness exacerbated by hostile surroundings and a siege-like situation,
etc.)

Despite recent increases the rates of agricultural progress in
Europe and Japan have been considerably slower than those of
Mexico and Israel. However, given its natural and historic conditions
and bearing in mind the most recent agricultural advances, Cuba
offers the possibility of extraordinary progress, stemming mainly
from four factors, which are examined below.

3. Increases and improvements in irrigation, genetics, pangola grass, plantings

Cuba has an average annual rainfall of a hundred and forty centimeters. In principle this is enough for agricultural yields, but the
rainfall is unevenly distributed: during some months – for example,
June 1969 – there may be more than forty centimeters of rain, and
pronounced dry spells have three times in eleven years reduced
sugarcane crops by twenty to thirty-five per cent. Studies by the

Institute of Water Resources have shown that, by accumulating runoffs and pumping all the available underground reservoirs of water, about twenty-two billion cubic meters of water could be obtained daily: enough to irrigate almost all Cuba's agricultural land, albeit at variable rates. However, the dams in existence before the revolution accumulated only a meager thirty million cubic meters, mostly for urban use. To this was added some riverbank and underground pumping, mostly for use in rice paddies, truck farms, and cattle watering. In June 1969 one billion cubic meters had already been stored up, and works under construction were soon to make it possible to store another billion – and pumping of underground sources was developing very rapidly. But more care should have been taken not to salt the ground water by pumping too close to the sea; provision should also have been made to protect the outlets of drainage canals from sea water by installing exit sluices. Because this protection was lacking, sea water reached for miles inland, salting large areas.

In the field of genetics two spectacular advances stand out. Rice strains developed in scientific experiments at the Los Banos International Institute of Rice Growing, near Manilla in the Philippines, now make it possible to achieve in tropical areas the very large rice yield that was hitherto reserved to Mediterranean climates. Under large-scale cultivation Honduras and Blue Bonnet varieties rarely returned more than three tons of paddy to the hectare; however, with the new IR8 strain and an increased dose of fertilizer, especially nitrates, six to seven tons can be harvested if the paddies are carefully tended. New strains are even more promising, and Cuba is rapidly increasing its small acreage of IR160, 480, etc. On May 26, 1969 Castro unhesitatingly announced: "We are on the way toward the development of the most modern rice paddies in the world, with a per-man productivity superior to that in the United States!" As we shall see, he was exaggerating.

The second advance in genetics concerns cattle. Cuba's herds are largely composed of zebu cows, which are reasonably resistant to the tropical climate, excellent meat producers, but poor milkers, yielding only 750 to 900 liters a year on a national average, including what the calf drinks. Initially, high producing Canadian Holsteins were introduced at great expense; they were not always suitably fed and they had trouble adjusting to the Cuban environment. But the rapid and widespread introduction of artificial insemination has directed current efforts toward the use of pedigree Holstein bulls to develop a hybrid herd, the famous F1s.* When they are well cared for, for example in the small dairy farms near Havana, they can produce from 2500 to 3000 liters of milk annually after the first lactation, and significantly more after the second.

In Cuba natural tropical prairies are generally, even in rich soils, disconcertingly poor. The introduction of guinea grass (*panicum maximum*) at the beginning of this century made for considerable improvement; better still, as far as milch cows are concerned, was the introduction of pangola grass (*digitaria decumbens*), which is more abundant, richer in proteins, and has a faster growth rate. Irrigation, fertilizer, and the supplementary use of molasses from the sugar refineries make it possible to nourish three to four cows for an entire year on a hectare of good pangola grass, without additional concentrates. And this offers the potential of more milk per hectare than is possible even in the best Normandy meadows. Stock farming in Cuba – which boasts rich Matanzas clays and a marginal tropical climate much superior to that of the average tropical country – is no longer handicapped in relation to countries in temperate climates. These are factors of primary importance for those who know how to make use of them.

Finally, and this is especially true since 1968, planting has developed at a rapidly accelerating pace. The plan then was to plant 270,000 hectares of citrus fruits,† and reach a maximum annual production goal of five million tons. (Less than 200,000 tons were obtained in 1969.) Cattura coffees were planted all over Cuba, especially near the cities, even in gardens ("everyone has to produce his own coffee supply"), but conditions were not always favorable: a favourite planting place was in the temporary spaces in orchards, from which the coffee plants would have to be uprooted when the fruit trees grew large. For permanent, long-term planting the Nuevo Mundo variety was preferred, but it couldn't be planted everywhere initially because not enough seed was available. (Since this variety has been cultivated in Brazil for the last fifteen years at least, the effort to *find* seed may have been inadequate.)

* Scientific popularization is well handled in Cuba: almost everyone in the country knows what F1 stands for. It must, however, be pointed out that among the Cuban people it sometimes tends to be scornfully applied to people of mixed African and white blood. Racism is on the retreat, but it dies hard.

† It was said that 10·7 million citrus plants were set out in 1967, which would account for 32,000 hectares. But the difference between the area planted in citrus trees on April 25, 1967 and February 10, 1968, was only 3323 hectares!

And pineapple cultivation is finally increasing. By June 1969, fifty-five million slips of "smooth Cayenne" had been planted in close double rows under a black polyethylene covering, a technique I had recommended in 1960 after a visit to Martinique.

During the Tenth Regional FAO Conference, held in Jamaica in December 1968, Carlos Rafael Rodriguez had the easy task of outlining the various aspects of Cuba's enormous agricultural effort. The country invests twenty-five to thirty per cent of its gross national product, and the largest part goes to agriculture – this in strong contrast with the future development of South America as outlined in the FAO world plan (1962–85).

According to the FAO plan, during the 1962–85 period South America would irrigate 3·5 million hectares of new land, or 160,000 hectares annually. It should be remembered that Central and South America, with 250 million inhabitants and more than seventeen million square kilometers, is about thirty times more populated and 150 times larger than Cuba. In 1968 and 1969, said Rodriguez, Cuba would irrigate 325,000 hectares, and plans called for the irrigation of 300,000 hectares of new land annually between 1970 and 1975 – in other words, 1·8 million in six years! During these twenty-three years Latin America hopes to clear thirty-five million hectares, or 1·3 million annually. Plans called for fifteen million to be cleared in the next ten years, thereby augmenting the arable area by fifteen per cent and making it about 100 million hectares. In 1967 alone Cuba cleared 300,000 hectares, and in the ten-year 1969–79 period it planned to increase the amount of land under cultivation from 4 to 6·7 million hectares: in other words sixty-five per cent in ten years.

By 1975 South America *in toto* hopes to be using two million tons of material containing fertilizers. By 1968 Cuba was already using half a million tons – in other words a quarter of that. By 1975, according to Castro, Cuba "will never use less than a million tons in net content, in other words more than half the amount of fertilizer that the FAO suggests for all South America." (Castro also said that by that year Cuba should also have at least 40,000 kilometers of paved roads – a kilometer for each two square kilometers of agricultural area.)

The famous Alliance for Progress, which was to "develop" South America within the context of its only barely reformed structures, is now very dead, officially buried by its godfather the United States.

Cuba's progress, on the other hand, can hardly be denied. Still, before drawing any conclusions, we must examine more closely the future efficacy of the tremendous investments made in the 1960s.

4. Special plans

In many traditional ways the Cuban state farm has remained a diversified agricultural operation. Cubans nevertheless studied the most modern cultivation techniques (those of the United States, with large-scale industrial agriculture able, for example, to use airplanes to sow seed and spread fertilizer, herbicides, pesticides, etc.). Then, toward the end of 1967, it was decided to extend the concept of the special plans* and establish them on a national basis. As we have seen, efforts were made to establish the alimentary autonomy of each province, so that both the distance that products had to be shipped and the amount of spoilage en route could be reduced. Next, attempts were made to localize the production of prime materials near the processing plants, if not near the ports from which they would be exported. All in all, the aim was to multiply the types of complex resembling the big sugarcane plantations linked to their central refineries.

We have already noted the top priority given once more to sugar; next in priority came the production of eggs, dairy products, and export crops – especially citrus fruit, coffee, and pineapples; last came meat, and food crops for local needs. On to this general canvas, sketched in by the political bureau and detailed by the Central Planning Committee, was superimposed an island-wide crop diversity according to soil, topography, and water. In this way each province and each region is divided into a certain number of plans. This will give the island a very special physiognomy; the effect of it can already be seen in the vicinity of the capital.

The irrigable low plains – on the south side of the island, especially in the Cauto valley in Oriente province – already grew some rice. The paddies were now to be increased by draining swamps, constructing irrigation and (sometimes) drainage works. The fairly flat rich plains situated somewhat higher (often of Matanzas or Havana clays) were to be planted with additional sugarcane so that this crop could be progressively withdrawn from the hilly areas where planting and especially harvesting cannot be mechanized. The

* See above, p. 33.

deeper soils were to be planted with citrus – even if they are sandy, as is the case of the grapefruit lands of the Isle of Pines – or more Nuevo Mundo coffee, bananas, etc. The shallower soils were to be planted with pineapple and other fruit trees, especially mangos. A *small* provision was to be made for tubers, garden crops for on-the-spot use, and winter vegetables for export.

On the hilly lands crops were to be replaced by pastures – native and imported – for milch cows and meat cattle. There was also to be pasture on moderate mountain slopes. The planned reforestation theoretically was carried out only on the poorest lands and this did not make for success. (Half the trees died; only half the remaining will be of any use.) Still, newly cultivated land is often protected by a planting of windbreaks and hedges which are a form of narrow-band reforestation – not much, but precious.

The plans also had to take into account the rapid drop in the numbers of farm workers, for this threatened the potential coffee and citrus harvests. An unusual solution to this problem was proposed. Until the 1960s Cuban children on the farms were treated as shop apprentices often are – the tendency being to give them the least agreeable jobs, which teach them little: weeding, carrying, picking up fallen fruit, and so on. Now the idea was to establish a junior high school for five hundred young students in the vicinity of each large citrus plantation. Trained adults would take care of planting, pruning, processing, etc., but the harvesting, still a manual operation, would be done by these young adolescents on a "half-work, half-study" basis. This proposal took account of the fact that Cuba's very faulty organization of adult male labor makes it proportionately more and more necessary to rely on the labor of adolescents and women.

What happened to the special plans? The history of these costly "Fidel plans" is a chronicle more of failures than successes. In 1960 I had hesitated to draw Castro's attention to the excessive cost of raising crocodiles at La Cienaga de Zapata; it was a whim of his that struck me as unimportant. I had hoped to retain influence on larger issues by not angering him over a minor point, but I was mistaken.

What about the Pinares de Mayari plan for garden farming? The new farms were established on ferruginous land that does not retain water, is subject to erosion, and is in other respects unsuitable to garden farming. Vegetables were successfully raised in the alluvial bottoms, but the rest of the soil filters too easily and lacks water.

Thousands of truckloads of soil were brought in, miles of piping were installed, handsome stables were built (despite the lack of fodder). It is hard to imagine how this could possibly have worked. The land was undergoing laterization and should not have been tampered with – pine forests would be more suitable for it. The coffee plan for San Andres de Caiguanabo in the Pinar del Rio province – where it was planned to establish communism immediately – has also failed. East of Havana, on the chalky, non-irrigable hills, I saw coffee plants that got hardly more than a meter of rainfall a year, with long stretches of dry months. And the Banao de las Villas plan for strawberries, grapevines, asparagus, garlic, and onions failed in 1967.

There had been a lot of boasting about cultivating grapes in Cuba. In 1969 I saw dozens of acres of sad-looking vineyards that had been planted on black, impermeable clays in the Bayamo area. (Later we shall note the failure of bananas and sugarcane in such soils.) Near Sancti Spiritus the better drained hills were planted with vines, but when I was there several pounds of fertilizer had been spread right up against each vine-stock and would surely burn it after the first rainfall. (I advised that it be spread broadcast over the entire vineyard, and I hope this was done.) Immense plans for raising goats and then rabbits were undertaken in 1965 and 1966; later they were more or less abandoned. In 1967–8 pigeon peas were planted over the entire island, but the results were meager and the cattle refused them – as did people. The tropical *kudzu* (vine) didn't result in the hoped-for miracle crops. And we will see how the large plantings begun in 1968 – citrus fruits, coffee, pineapples, bananas – were not always carried out under the best conditions.

It would be an exaggeration to say that everything has failed. As I have said, the artificial insemination program is a great success; the results of correctly established pangola prairies are good (although costly); the irrigation works are very promising, in spite of some errors; IR8 rice is also a success. Many of these projects were worth while, and the failures are due to the fact that they were impetuously launched on too vast a scale by the *líder maximo*.

5. Medical care and education

I bowed very low to the young lady doctor of the Victorino rural clinic. This young slip of a woman, handicapped by the aftermath of a polio attack, her medical studies scarcely over, ran a clinic in the

Sierra Maestra with the help of three nurses serving ten thousand people. Her workload was soon to be cut when other clinics opened, but when I saw her she had had eighty-four consultations that day, half of them in pediatrics. (A maternity service was attached to the clinic.) Here finally was a socialized medicine, entirely free of the spirit of lucre that too often taints the devotion of doctors in so-called developed countries.

Drs Molina and Rojas Ochon explained to me that of the 6300 doctors practicing in Cuba in January 1959, a little more than 2500 had left, particularly during the 1961-5 period. Many of these were the older doctors, often the more experienced specialists and medical-school professors. A good part of this loss was made up by foreign doctors, often Latin Americans, and in July 1969 there were already 7200 Cuban doctors – more than there had been in 1958. But most of these were young, and there was still a persistent lack of specialists. It was therefore decided to train 2000 additional specialists by 1971. "The most difficult thing will be to make up for the loss of quality."

The small rural clinics, often with no more than a dozen beds, and the city polyclinics represent great progress. Initial efforts made it possible to wipe out malaria (13,500 cases in 1962 but only four in 1968, all from abroad) and polio, and also made for great progress against dysentery, gastroenteritis, and other intestinal infections. A campaign is now under way to prevent deaths from cancer of the uterus by spotting it in its early stages. But many problems touching on drinking water, sewage disposal, and technical personnel still remain to be solved. . . .

The Cuban mortality rate is already very low: seven per thousand. This is partially due to the fact that the population is very young; forty-six per cent of all Cubans are below the age of fifteen. The infant mortality rate is only four per cent. The birth rate was officially set at twenty-nine per thousand inhabitants, but many people think that the latest census will show it to be higher.

However, in mid-1969 it was said that since October 1965 more than 50,000 people had left Cuba annually – as many as died each year. These were people who could not or would not adapt to the new regime – not only members of the middle class but workers and even some disillusioned young people who had been members of the Party. Since April 1971 it has been forbidden to leave Cuba at all.

Though contraception and abortion are legal they are not encouraged; systematic Malthusianism is rejected. But it is estimated that urbanization, the increased number of women working, and obligatory military service have significantly lowered the birth rate since 1965, and that this trend will continue.

By the summer of 1969 44,000 children were already being taken care of in 365 day-care centers. If women must work, the children must be taken care of during the day. And children (like the scholarship students lodged in the fancy Havana villas) are the true favorites of the government and are very well treated from all points of view.

Cuban officials have given us impressive figures in educational matters: the number of students and teachers in primary, secondary, and higher education has rapidly multiplied. The new idea – schools that will be permanently established near the fields and relate study to manual labor, thereby lowering the barriers that exist in other countries between intellectual and manual work – is in principle a very good one, but it must be well applied. As in China, agricultural specialists, peasants, and workers, as well as teachers, should participate in planning the programs, if not in running the schools. But thinking in this field remains too authoritarian.

More agricultural cadres are being trained in Cuba than anywhere else in the Third World. The number of those pursuing technical agricultural studies has doubled in two years, going from 17,000 to 33,000 students – 16,000 of whom have reached the secondary level – in twenty-six study centers. In 1967 and 1968 1500 middle-level agronomists and 300 specialists in artificial insemination graduated. There is also widespread training of agronomists at the university level, but it has led to neither the number (only 150 a year) nor the quality necessary.

In most countries there is an increasing tendency to make the community responsible for at least the major proportion of health and education expenses. But, as we have seen, Cuba's conception of communism goes considerably further in both the political and the economic sector. The time has come to outline the principal instruments for Cuba's transition to communism, which is already being proclaimed as in progress.

6. The Party: designated rather than elected?

The Cuban Communist Party, itself in the process of development, is the leader. A Central Committee (we will come back to this) took over the national direction of the United Party of the Socialist Revolution; in the beginning, it was smaller. Next comes the

Secretariat of the Central Committee, an eight-man politbureau including President Dorticós and Major Guillermo Garcia (who is also leader of Cuba's largest province, Oriente). The innermost group, which makes the essential decisions, is the five-man secretariat of this political bureau: Fidel Castro, Raul Castro, Armando Hart, Blas Roca, and Carlos Rafael Rodriguez.

Each of Cuba's six provinces has a Party committee. In addition there are two special committees for Havana and the Isle of Youth (formerly the Isle of Pines). Then come the regional and municipal committees; then the base cells in the production units. Units of national importance – such as the ministries, the university, nationwide industries – are managed directly by the Central Committee and not by any local leadership.

The recent trend is to send top-level political leaders, members of the Central Committee, to take charge of provinces, important regions, and major production plans. This is done so that the people can more easily come into contact with the country's highest officials, and so that the latter have a good grasp of the real situation within the country. As a result, Major Curbelo is in charge of a region and of the "Camagüey Rectangle" Plan; Faustino Perez runs the Sancti Spiritus region. In Havana, Jesus Betancourt, first provincial secretary, is also in charge of provincial agriculture. Juan Almeida is the Party delegate to the Ministry of Construction, and it takes up all basic problems with him.

In principle the Party is recruited from among the exemplary or avant-garde workers, themselves elected by the mass and chosen for their devotion, their assiduousness in productive labor, their good fellowship, etc. The assemblies that designate them are valid only if they include three-quarters of the workers in the given unit. Militants who are already members of the Party therefore discuss among themselves matters concerning these "exemplaries" and their possible deficiencies. The result is that members of *this* group are the ones who really decide who may join the Party; the names are then presented to the assemblies for nomination by acclamation.

Designation is thus rapidly being substituted for election, thereby emphasizing a power that comes from the top rather than the base. If he commits errors a member is judged by his cell. In addition, "cadres in important positions [at the central and provincial echelons] are designated by the political bureau." Is this still the democratic centralism corrected by popular control that Lenin advocated? The provincial committee incorporates among its members those comrades ratified, rather than designated, by the electors; since there are often twenty-five candidates for twenty places, the electors' option is severely limited.

In the army, the police, and the ministries leadership is completely designated, since these groups are concerned with problems of defense and security that cannot be exposed in public.

7. The state: subordinated to the Party?

Osvaldo Dorticós, President of the Cuban Republic, is not the number one man in Cuba. We already know that this place belongs to Fidel Castro, Prime Minister of the revolutionary government but also commander-in-chief of the armed revolutionary forces and First Secretary of the Cuban Communist Party. Any one of his three functions would be enough to occupy a very active man. Castro is also super-Minister of Agriculture; a subject he knows quite a bit about although he too is quite capable of making errors with fearful consequences, given his uncontrolled power.

Cuba is simultaneously administered by ministries of the classical kind and national agencies which are often economic, such as the Agriculture and Animal Husbandry Development, the Fishing and Forest Institute; *Diname*, which allocates machinery; *Ceseta*, which maintains it; *Acopio*, which is supposed to collect agricultural products; the National Poultry Board; *Cubatabacco*, etc. There are also cultural bodies – institutes of cinema, literature, friendship with other peoples (responsible for the reception of foreign guests), the National Council of Culture and Education, the Casa de las Americas, etc. In principle, Havana University should be attached to the National Education Council; in practice, it is autonomous, especially since the Rector has direct access to Castro, who appointed to this essential post a man in whom he has every confidence.

This last phrase is a key factor in the delegation of power in Cuba. As an official, one either has, or one has lost, Castro's confidence. To a great extent the assignment of responsibility depends on personal connections. Leadership of the economy's essential agencies is placed in the hands of men in whom "the boss" has confidence. And each ministry and each national agency creates provincial and sometimes regional organizations in the same manner.

Relations between the Party and the state have undergone various changes in fortune. In 1960–1, before it had attained a level of capacity that would make such intervention efficacious, the Party all too often substituted for the state (as is still in some degree the case in the Soviet Union). The Party and the state were then still somewhat separate. Now an attempt is being made for the Party to make the big decisions, the basic orientations, provided that it no longer interferes with daily decisions, which are left to the administrative organs. The director of a factory or a plan is alone responsible; he is permanently aided by the Party cell, which is supposed to support and assist him without over-riding his responsibility.

[A more recent trend consists in often confiding corresponding functions in the Party and in administration to the same man. No attempts are being made to separate the Soviet and the Party, as in the USSR.] Companero Hermes Herrera – who was my guide in Cuba during my June–July 1969 visit and who explained to me these various mechanisms of the Party, the state, of planification, etc. – is director of the Institute of Economy of Havana University; he is also the secretary of the Institute's Party cell. He is also the first secretary of the Party section of the university. Miguel Martin, administrative leader of the Holguin region (in Oriente province), is also first secretary of the Party regional section, etc. Under these circumstances, the organizer and the inspector are one and the same. In principle there are therefore no more contradictions, but are not contradictions the very motor of the system? Is this not an orientation toward an even more authoritarian structure? "Fidel Castro will decide on the orientation of the future," concluded Hermes Herrera. All in all, Cuba's political and administrative structures are in constant evolution, and in Cuba pragmatism always claims domination over dogmatism. This allows Castro to remain the big boss, omnipresent if not omniscient.

Note should be taken of the diminishing role of the unions, which are perhaps due to disappear entirely. There is no fondness for their traditional oppositional role, since now the unions can be opposed only to the state employer, and the state is (in principle) the state of the workers. Considerably more importance is therefore given to the avant-garde workers' movement. But is that a real elite? This is a basic question against which all the communist parties in the world stumble.

8. The Central Planning Committee and the plan

The Central Planning Committee is – or was? – the command post of the Cuban economy: both the Ministry of Finance and the universal super-Ministry of the Economy, deciding not only on fundamental policy but on means of production. In agriculture it tries to make national objectives compatible with various potentialities, regional particularities, and so on; and closely links, for example, the agriculture plan to user industries (foods, fibers) and supplier industries (fertilizers, materials). The Committee's machinery division supplies production units with the necessary equipment; its foreign commerce division takes care of imports and exports; the transport division also plays its essential and difficult role. All in all the Central Planning Committee is the major coordinating organism for all units of production, transport, conversion, distribution, and national import-export. In January of each year it begins to establish the principal production objectives for the coming year on the basis of national directives decided on by the political authorities. Though each annual plan is based on scientific data, the Committee knows that it cannot develop an optimum scientific plan. At any given moment a choice takes on a certain arbitrary character, is affected by social and psychological factors, foreign relations, etc. A choice of a political nature is obviously called for. Politics increasingly dominate the makeup of the plan; the Committee seems to be reduced to an organ for documentation on the one hand, and control of policy execution on the other.

The plan is further broken down on the provincial level and brought into line as far as possible with the goals proposed by the province. Contracts are worked out with factories – and at this point the crucial problem of the labor pool assumes importance. The regular workers come within the province of the Ministry of Labor. But there are years when not enough are available, and volunteer workers must be mobilized, notably by the Confederation of Cuban Workers, the Young Communist League, the various ministries, the Federation of Women, etc.

After taking into consideration all information on available resources, the political leadership and the government work out and proclaim the national plan developed by the Planning Committee; this includes breakdowns by province, region, and production unit. At the same time, each unit is assigned the resources necessary for realization of the plan. In each province a delegate of the political bureau periodically checks on the situation, supervises execution of the plan, and tries to improve quality, giving very special attention to the agricultural sector. The national agencies already referred to get busy constructing roads, dams, and canals; they transport, supply, repair. . . .

The complexity of this planning increases the closer one gets to the base of the economy, which has also collaborated in development of the plan. Though those at the summit provide the broad outline, the base participates – in its assignment of which areas are to be planted, let us say – in the multiple details of actual execution. These activities lead to certain corrections in the plan, but they are only minor ones because on the whole the emphasis of movement is from top to bottom, and the base intervenes in the development of plans less than it did in 1964–6. The structure appears to be more hierarchized, more authoritarian. Each production unit, each agricultural plan, receives its own resources and uses them as it sees fit. But decisions about important materials are made at the regional or even provincial level.

9. Money retreats before free services and scarcities

Money plays a considerably less significant role in Cuba than in other socialist countries; however, its rapid decline in importance has both positive and negative aspects.

The positive aspect is represented by Cuba's extension of services available free to its citizens – a hundred per cent of medical services at its clinics and hospitals (though some prefer private medical consultation), and the same for all levels of education (even school supplies and books are free, although in a limited quantity).* Scholarship holders, mostly from rural areas, are maintained entirely at state expense. Rent will be free, in most cases, after 1972. Water, telephone service, etc, are also free.

The role of money is also limited not only by the low fixed prices on all daily expenses such as food or transportation, but also and especially by the general lack of everything, by the universal ration-

---

* Students are of course called on to perform a certain amount of manual labor. I consider this a positive factor too, if only because it is a demonstration of the respect which Cuba's future "elite" thereby accords manual labor – although this would be true only to the extent that the practice does not compromise the quality of the education.

ing and the very pronounced scarcity of consumer goods and many foods. None of this represents a transition toward a communism of abundance, but it may be a transition toward that communism of austerity evoked by the Chinese.

There is a desire to eliminate privation quickly in Cuba, but the high investment rate, the American blockade, the revolution's enormous initial difficulties, and the country's relative underdevelopment must be kept in mind. Yet is a rapid abandonment of material incentives the best way to overcome quickly these formidable obstacles? This does not seem to be the opinion of Rodriguez, who has emphasized that Che Guevara himself acknowledged the necessity of certain incentives. Yet an important step in the direction of renouncing incentives was taken in 1968, when there was increasingly widespread refusal to pay overtime. Was this always spontaneous? It seems doubtful, but we shall return to this point. First we will have to abandon these lovely visions of the future and return to earth, where at the beginning of the 1970s Cuba was struggling against many difficulties.

4

The Years of Hard Facts*
1968-71

DURING my first days in Cuba in 1969 I believed that an imminent and fairly rapid transition to a communist society without marked privation was possible. I expressed reservations about the feasibility of the announced fifteen per cent annual increases in agricultural production over the next twelve years, but there was something convincing in the assurances Castro gave me on the afternoon and evening of Sunday June 29 when we made an inspection tour together. The F1 cows grazed in fine pangola pasture, and they seemed to be in good health.† Castro told me that at the Nina Bonita genetic center, where he went almost every day, sixteen cows were nourished on about 1·6 hectares of pasture; in other words ten cows to the hectare! (An expert told me that if it were paced out this pasture would actually be equivalent to 2·5 hectares; these F1s also receive as much concentrated food as they can eat, and this amounts to half their ration. The real situation therefore corresponds to nine or ten cows on 2·5 hectares – in other words four cows to the hectare, which is pretty good.)

I was prepared to believe in the magnificent results obtained with the "miracle" rice IR8 developed in the Philippines. And indeed this rice splendidly confirmed its promise in Cuba. But the succeeding strains, notably IR160 and IR480, were proclaimed as superior before adequate testing. Experiments in raising rice without submersion, by aspersion watering, suggested the possibility of saving the enormous, indeed wasteful, amounts of water required in traditional rice culture; Castro justifiably emphasizes

---

* On January 2 Castro baptizes every year with a name, which then becomes the watchword for that year: 1969 was the Year of Decisive Effort, a term that implies a worrying sort of deadline.

† Some cowsheds had air conditioning, an expense for which nobody could indicate an economic return. The most modern technique is not always the most economical.

that with the traditional procedures water is the most expensive of weed-killers.

Much of the sugarcane planting made it possible to anticipate crops of a size that would dwarf those of 1960, to say nothing of 1963. Some areas promised as much as two hundred tons of cane per hectare, in other words twenty-four tons of sugar, if the refineries could get a twelve per cent net return.*

What impressed me most was the total change in the immediate environs of the capital and even the whole province of Havana in comparison with what I had seen in 1960 and 1963. Where once a few beautiful luxury estates had been sandwiched between peasant farms of varying importance – more often, between stretches of waste land or natural pastures close to being waste land – now young orchards were to be found. Further on were carefully tended dairy farms with small pangola pastures surrounded by white picket fences. Traveling with Castro I sometimes had the impression that I was visiting Cuba with its owner, who was showing off its fields and pastures, its cows if not its men. The impression was not wholly erroneous, since Castro is in fact the overall manager of an enormous production enterprise, a role of which he is profoundly aware, as his speeches show. In any event, a big landowner always takes better care of the lands near his house than of those portions further off. I found this to be true in China where, in the interval between my 1955 and 1965 visits, the outskirts of large cities such as Peking and Shanghai had undergone a greater transformation than had the rest of the agricultural landscape.

As a result of Castro's attention to my comments, I sent him a daily summary of my principal observations. In my very first note I praised the enormous change in the landscape around Havana and noted that only in China had I ever seen such a profound transformation in a countryside. But I pointed out that this gigantic effort had only modestly increased Chinese harvests, that the results were disproportionate to the massive investment. I had attributed this disparity primarily to lack of fertilizer and secondly to a reduction in the intensity of peasant efforts following the creation of the People's Communes, initially disliked by most Chinese peasants. But Cuba hardly lacks fertilizer. When in a euphoria brought on by my first favorable impression I told

---

* In France, when beet sugar yields six to eight tons to the hectare it is considered a very good return.

Castro that he might well beat all records for agricultural progress in the socialist camp, he looked rather dubious. "You really think so?" he asked. With an effort at candor that he is still sometimes capable of, he added, "Revolution is not easy, you know."

1. Scarcity and consumer goods

Let me emphasize again that nowhere in Cuba have I encountered the extreme poverty one sees in parts of Mexico, in many regions in northeastern Brazil, or in much of the Andes from Colombia and Peru to Bolivia. Nobody is starving, but austerity reigns and food shortages are as severe as they were in 1962, if not more so.

Basic food rations and local transportation are very cheap, and salaries have been raised. Most Cubans want to spend their money quickly, and are not inclined to save it or invest it – nor are they urged to do so, since this would require the promise of interest, which is heresy. But they have little opportunity to do so. When an occasion does arise, everybody rushes to take advantage of it, and as a result the queues keep growing and growing. At official ration outlets an attempt has been made to reduce the queues by dividing consumers into groups. But the lines grow anyway because those who come first get first choice and are sure of getting something. In one small city people waited in the rain all night for espadrilles; it turned out that only two pairs were available!

Since in some circles there is a great deal of money – monthly salaries range from eighty-five to nine hundred pesos – gross inequalities are maintained. Excess money can only be spent in restaurants or on the black market. A simple meal of soup, spaghetti, ice cream, coffee, and beer costs 4·5 pesos, which means that a minimum salary would only pay for nineteen of these meals a month. A good meal costs more than twice as much. The competition to spend the money on these limited outlets continues. To eat in a restaurant, where no ration coupons are required, people wait unprotestingly for an hour or two hours, and this was true in all the cities I visited. Some evenings in Havana you can wait in a queue for as long as three hours to get an ice cream. (It is by the way as good as ever. The capitalist manufacturer is still in Cuba, where he enjoys friendly attentions and even some privileges.) Children are sometimes dressed in bits of old sacking, and young girls are ashamed of their tattered clothing. The old

section of Havana used to be so gay! We are well rid of the
prostitution, but not everything about the pre-revolutionary Havana
was bad. Now you stand in line for the movies, for a carriage ride
around Holguin, to get a seat in a café that sells neither coffee nor
beer, but only lemonade or diluted fruit drinks. You queue for the
bus, which comes infrequently at best. Because salaries have risen
faster than production and imported consumer goods have been
reduced to a trickle, these endless queues result in unproductive
fatigue for the workers and a lower standard of living.

Economic laws sometimes take a fiendish revenge. Given the same
basic resources, a better apportionment of available funds and a
better organization of distribution could have eliminated or at least
reduced this problem. The Soviet Union paid heavily for forgetting
this economic truth, and its slowness to rediscover it harmed the
country's rate of progress. Does Cuba really have to repeat all the
economic errors of the socialist camp?

A housewife said to me, "You must write about how we lack
everything. Many ration coupons are not honored. Chicken is
reserved for invalids and pregnant women. My neighbor's son is
almost two, and she still hasn't got the chicken due her when she
was pregnant. I haven't had a pair of shoes since 1963. Some of
my neighbors managed to get a pair, but how they had to wait!
For four years now no trousers – just one pair a year given out with
a shirt at the labor centers. If you cook pork the whole neighborhood can smell it, and if the local Revolutionary Defense Committee
hears about it, they denounce you. By the end of the month all
you've got to wash yourself with is some kind of horrible
detergent. The monthly ration of beans is just enough for three
meals [Cubans are often not very farsighted]. If you have a lot of
children and get the minimum salary of eighty-five pesos, you can't
even think of buying extras. Pizza costs 1·20 pesos, a small bottle of
beer – when there is any – comes to ·80 pesos, a *perro caliento* costs
·40 pesos, and the price is ·60 if cheese is added. If you miss a day's
work, you're not paid. With a doctor's certificate, you get a third of
your pay."

In public everybody is for Castro; in private his partisans are less
numerous. Everybody goes to the demonstrations in the Plaza de la
Revolucion. You leave from wherever you work and it's obligatory.*

---

* On May 20, 1960, it was really spontaneous. On July 14, 1969, it was mostly
a question of reservist battalions.

If the truck stops along the way, many people slip away. Sometimes melons and oranges are sold in the Plaza. What a windfall! Barriers are speedily set up and the endless lines form. During the main speech sale is suspended, and those who were getting close to the treasure become angry. "One hundred years of struggle," goes the slogan; "plus ten years of lies," add the people.

Anybody who works in a factory is fed at the canteen, and in this way his ration is supplemented. But a ladleful of corn mush is most likely to be the meal of the young people of the Columna, whereas high officials get chicken and rice, avocados, cigars, and coffee. A foreign guest is entitled to a banquet. But how difficult things are for fatherless families, for those no longer young, and for the elderly housewife!

2. Unkept promises

In 1969 foreigners and Cubans alike viewed me with astonishment when I argued that there were concrete and tangible possibilities for rapidly increasing Cuban agricultural production, even though the percentage increases announced by Castro were wholly incredible. A majority of the diplomatic corps in Havana, even from eastern Europe, privately believes that the Cuban economy is headed for catastrophe. I nevertheless hesitated – and still do hesitate – to accept such a conclusion. A careful examination of all the positive factors encourages more optimism. In addition, I had never believed the promises made by the Cuban government in earlier years and don't set much store by the promises made now.

In May 1967 Castro addressed the peasants attending the second – and probably last – congress of the National Association of Small Farmers. He extolled the advantages of large-scale agriculture and sharply attacked the *microfundia*. This view, which has its wisdom as I have argued earlier, unhappily had prevented him from drawing on peasant farming knowledge, a valuable source of information for those who know how to make use of it without following it in all details. It had led him into the errors of the special plans, as well as into many other mistakes.

Some of the delegates attempted a timid defense of those small farmers who operated efficiently. Castro supported his point of view with only marginal examples, citing cases of extreme poverty in the Sierra Maestra. He sensibly advised against planting bananas on the steep slopes of those historic mountains, where each planting precipitates erosion; the state *granjas*, he explained, were going to plant 2000 *caballerias* (27,000 hectares) of bananas in Oriente province alone, and full production was expected by 1969. "Then we'll have so many bananas that we won't sell them to you, we'll *give* them to you." He added that Oriente province would also be producing 1·3 million liters of milk daily by 1969.

I inspected Oriente province in July 1969, and in the low Cauto valley, on either side of the island's central road, I saw mile upon mile of banana plantations where the trees were dying because they had been planted in badly drained soil where the water table was tainted with magnesium salts. The average peasant would have avoided this gross error; was it therefore admissible in a state enterprise, whose only justification is in its technical superiority? At the provincial agricultural command post I was told that 4350 hectares of state-grown banana trees were still in good shape: less than one-sixth of what Castro had promised in 1967. Milk production there was estimated at 310,000 liters daily, less than one-quarter of the promised goal. (Castro admitted on July 26, 1970 that in the first half of 1970 Cuban milk production decreased by one-fourth.) Luckily, the ever-prudent Sierra peasants had planted their own bananas. If they hadn't, they wouldn't even have been able to *buy* a single banana, since there were only enough to meet established priorities – ill people and children, for the most part – and this in a land where bananas are not a luxury item but a daily staple preferred to bread.

On that same day in May 1967 Castro had promised the construction of 100,000 housing units annually after 1970 – a remarkable achievement were it possible. In the summer of 1969 I was told that Cuba would complete about 24,000 units that year – still remarkable in comparison with 1958, when for the most part only luxury housing was being built. Expectations were that 28,000 housing units would be completed – with difficulty – in 1970: somewhat more than one-fourth of what had been promised.

Rents have been sharply reduced and fixed in relation to salaries. After 1970–2 they will for the most part be eliminated. Housing is progressively becoming the property of the assignee. This means that existing arrangements are perpetuated even in unfair instances: some bachelors may have many rooms while many young people who want to get married cannot find space to live. Each job transfer complicates the problem, and people are constantly looking for chances to exchange flats. The only people not bothered by this situation are top officials, for whom everything can always be arranged. The system leads not only to the perpetuation, but the accentuation of social injustices.

Since March 13, 1968 housing has been run by the nationalized enterprises, and this poses all sorts of problems – beginning with materials, painting, pipes, electrical wire, roofing, available workers. . . . A request for a simple repair must be made to the proper department, and then the waiting begins. Meanwhile Cuba's real-estate patrimony is rapidly deteriorating. The look of the old cities of Havana, Santiago de Cuba, Bayamo, Holguin, Camaguey is particularly dispiriting. Façades are crumbling, boards sometimes replace windowpanes. The investment in new construction may well be largely cancelled out by the losses that such dilapidation represents.

In late 1968 Castro promised in no uncertain terms to quadruple Cuban milk production in two years with a herd of seven million. When I read this announcement my few remaining hairs stood on end. True enough, with artificial insemination F_1 heifers are born en masse to zebu cows. Five hundred thousand would begin producing milk in 1970. If they all were good producers (let us say 3000 liters a year) that would mean 1·5 million additional tons of milk annually. By adding this to the present production of 800,000 tons, we arrive at a figure that is almost triple. I suppose that with a little imagination this can be considered as *quadrupled* production: Castro has lots of imagination.

The confusion between maximums and averages is classic in communist countries. And Castro often mistakes the conception of a project for its actual realization. Even 525,000 additional tons of milk per year – which given the current figures in 1967 was a reasonable assumption – could only be obtained by meeting a great number of prerequisites, beginning with improved pasturage. To improve the yield and raise the average production it would also have been necessary to eliminate twenty per cent of the F_1 heifers and concentrate on the ones that promise to be good milkers. Plans were to keep all the heifers, and this is a big mistake.

There are, however, some hopeful signs. Castro once sharply reproached my guides for not having shown me the Camillo Cienfuegos factory for nitrate fertilizers. The actual construction of the plant had served to train qualified workers and technical personnel, each new worker, whatever his qualifications, had received in addition cultural and technical "improvements." This was considered part of the brigade's daily work.* Whereas it had been thought that it would take 4000 workers three years to complete the installations, the 1600 workers, "who for the most part came on the job with no qualifications," were to finish the job in three years. "All the workers *participate* in the study and interpretation of the work they are carrying out." Let us salute this all too rare example and hope that this spirit of participation will not be thwarted.

3. The "revolutionary offensive" and the third agrarian reform of 1968

July 26, 1953 the attack on the Moncada barracks; March 13, 1957 the assault on Batista's presidential palace; January 2, 1959 the triumph of Castro's rebellion. On the anniversary of each of these historic dates Fidel Castro delivers an important speech; the March 13 one is often devoted to internal political problems. On March 13, 1968 Castro attacked the surviving remnants of private business and concentrated his fire on bars "haunted" by counter-revolutionaries, bars in which illegal alcohol was sold, bars that made enormous profits. He also castigated the little fried-food shops and insisted on their immediate nationalization.

The owners of these places were hardly angelic revolutionaries, but when they went, and when the last small shops and various services went too, an important supplementary food source disappeared that was often in addition an outlet for goods from the peasant farmers who lived on the outskirts of the city. Because state production was still unable to replace it, this meant that food was in even shorter supply. Black market supplies became extremely limited and their prices rose even higher. Everywhere, from Havana to Bayamo, vegetables, fruits, and clothing disappeared from the stores. The shortages, which had been bearable until then, suddenly became shocking and dramatic.

Other important commodities and services disappeared. For example, it became all but impossible to have certain kinds of repairs done. From now on one had to turn to state agencies. Unless you had connections the smallest painting job, the most minor plumbing or electrical repair became a "matter of state". All the small shops were turned over to local authorities, and the new management of them provoked many customer complaints. It should come as no

---

* See p. 98 for a description of the Che Guevara Brigade.

surprise that many small shopkeepers have joined the ranks of those trying to leave Cuba.

As for the third agrarian reform – a term that is not used and would not be acceptable in Cuba – the official history as told in propaganda sounds like a fairly tale. One day Castro suddenly appeared in the home of a poor peasant said to have been badly housed, badly equipped, and underproductive. He offered him a completely furnished new house free of charge; the peasant's fields would be cultivated by the state as part of a microplan established for each farm. Under the plan, each peasant family would keep two or three hectares to grow food, mostly tubers, for its own needs; the rest of the land would be planted with trees chosen for the region and maintained by volunteers mobilized in the city. The profits from this free planting and cultivation were theoretically to be the peasant's, but the future was left in shadow. This permits a change of basic orientation without the appearance of an about-face in policy – de Gaulle has his disciples.

That was the idea in 1968, but after 1969 it, too, was completely overhauled and changed. The peasant was still to retain ownership of the fields in which he raised crops for his own consumption, but all the rest of his property was integrated into state plans. The first two agrarian reforms had guaranteed the peasant's perpetual ownership; now he was theoretically to be indemnified for the land he turned over to the state. There was talk of eight hundred to a thousand pesos of *rent* for each *caballeria*; some said that the thousand pesos was more in the form of a purchase price paid by the state. It was therefore either a great deal of money or very little. From the few interviews I was able to arrange it appeared that the peasant thus expropriated (let's call things by their proper names) got, in addition to the furnished house, an annuity of an amount determined by his family needs.

Peasant acceptance of these propositions varied greatly and largely depended on the individual's previous situation. The peasant who worked his land little or badly accepted readily; those in the Havana area were urged to accept by their wives, as soon as the women saw that neighbors were being established in better housing. Their children attended school and often had no interest in becoming microfundists, but hoped rather to settle in the city; if they had to stay in the fields, they preferred to do so as technicians or tractor drivers.

To get a more detailed view of these extremely optimistic Marxist-

Santa Claus tableau, let's look into the situation of a few interested parties selected at random. The first peasant whose opinion I solicited about this solution answered, "*es bueno*," "it's fine" – in an unconvincing, hang-dog tone. Another, who cultivated about thirty hectares – mostly sugarcane – with a tractor, told me that between January and May he had delivered to the central refinery 1700 tons of cane raised by himself (aged seventy), his son (aged thirty-six), and three employees paid by him. As of July he had still not been paid for the cane, and he feared that he never would be. And the acreage left him for his own use was damp and could only be used for rain-fed rice. This man was a real farmer ("I've been farming for forty-five years, day in and day out"), who worked the land productively and efficiently and didn't want to leave it. His son was too old to change professions. Even in the presence of a Party official – who followed us unasked – the farmer made no attempt to hide his bitterness. Given his "reservations" about the authorities, he was afraid that he would never get the promised 120-peso annuity. I was told that some of his farmer friends had committed suicide. A new segment of peasant opinion was joining the opposition to the regime.

The maneuvers leading to this expropriation can be realistically summed up as follows. Until 1967 an ANAP examiner would, for statistical purposes, ask peasants about their planting plans. In 1967 the examiner would suggest desirable modifications in what the farmers intended to sow. In 1968 he gave them *orders* established according to the regional agricultural plan, which was now obligatory. A campaign was initiated to have all available production turned over to *Acopio*, the state commerce agency. At first presented as something that was to be done voluntarily, this delivery was soon made mandatory, and adherence was promoted by the publication of a list of fines for various infractions.

That same year the peasants were asked to understand that since the state farms were short of labor it would be nice if they would voluntarily make time to work on the *granjas*; shortly afterward, the peasant was forbidden to employ paid help on his own. His children were generally boarded at school, so this meant the peasant had to work the land unaided. At this point, many of them sold most of their land to the state.

The more efficient farmers managed to hang on. Then the government published a map on which the entire island was divided into agricultural plans (on previous maps private property was left

3

blank, official programs applying only to state property, as I was told at the Institute of Physical Planning). All peasants were now included in a plan, and they quickly came to be looked upon as intruders in it. They were politely asked to cede their land voluntarily to the state, which offered them jobs as workers in the nearest plan – though sometimes the plan was a bit farther away. . . . They retained the right to occupy their houses and to grow food for their own use, but only temporarily. Though some beautiful houses were built for them in the ex-urban belt around Havana (where there were foreign visitors!) it was obviously impossible to do the same everywhere. Some peasants continued to resist, saying that they had been cheated and super-cheated by Castro: "He told us so often that land would never be taken from a peasant! That the nation had contracted a debt of honor toward us. . . . "

And so, following the suppression of all private commerce and craftsmanship, the peasantry as such in turn disappeared, suddenly and without being consulted. To some extent they can be said to have been bought off. Some accepted the situation and some are better off, with their subsistence acreage and their houses. But the most industrious peasants, who already had houses and had accumulated some working capital, felt cheated, and many were unwilling to accept the situation.

One of the government's underlying reasons for these measures was no doubt to suppress the black market by eliminating the outlying peasant farms that supplied it. This might have been commendable if at the same time other sources of food supply had been created. Within Havana I saw small, well-kept vegetable gardens, occasionally in conjunction with a few livestock. (Three piglets were being raised on bread at a spot not far from 128th Street and 29th Avenue, but on a second visit I found that they had been eliminated for reasons of sanitation.) If every family that wanted to had been able to have a small garden plot, it could have raised a good portion of its own food.

If the intention had been to combat the individualistic spirit behind the vegetable patches, some arrangement could have been made for collective plantings by groups of city workers from the same office or factory. I even suggested a formula for "communist hectares," each hectare cultivated by about thirty workers and used to raise tubers, vegetables, bananas, papayas, and other quick growing fruit; the harvest could have been distributed among the producers, who would then have had the incentive of working for their families. If the idea is to establish a higher morality, to attach each individual to his family cell, he should be allowed to work for it *preferentially*.

Instead of the green belt for Havana I had proposed in June 1960 in my first report to Castro, in 1969 I found the outskirts of the city planted with orchards interspersed with coffee. Forced to plant only cane or coffee the peasants who had formerly supplied the city became ration consumers instead of providers. And the above project had been carried out with little preliminary study: the humid, rocky, or over-shallow soils were unsuitable for most fruits. And the coffee plants do not seem to have optimum growing conditions here, for the mean temperature is too high for them. Though the lemon trees have survived, part of the coffee plantings had to be torn up, especially along Via Monumental. June having been extremely rainy, the coffee plants looked green when I arrived, but I saw them rapidly turning yellow right up to the Protocolo, where I was lodged. During my stay, they even had to uproot the coffee plants from the rocky acreage that can be seen from the villa in which the Prime Minister's agricultural technical team works. Of course, these were only temporary plantings; nevertheless, the 50,000 workers who were mobilized to plant them in March–May 1969 seeing them uprooted, cannot but have felt that they had wasted a great deal of effort.*

The state vegetable crops that were supposed to fill the gap left by peasant production were also way behind. At the beginning of July the expected crop for Havana province amounted to less than 70,000 tons as against 90,000 in 1967, and even that was not a year of abundance.

In addition, part of the crop was for export (either fresh or canned). Fruit and vegetables had all but disappeared from non-priority rations in Havana. True, export is an absolute necessity. But I wonder whether this neglect of urban needs isn't another instance of a more or less unconscious and deep-buried desire to punish a somewhat decadent, bourgeois, and intellectual city that

---

* A group of city workers saw, near the plot they were working on, a grove of more or less abandoned mangos heavy with succulent fruits that weren't being gathered. They asked for permission to pick some so that the fruit wouldn't be lost. Permission was refused, but the next week soldiers came and gathered the more or less rotten mangoes for their pigs. Such things happen too often, and they end by irritating those subjected to unjust privations. Castro doesn't realize this because he suffers no privations.

is difficult to win over and that previously lived in a parasitical relationship to the rest of Cuba. Everything possible is being done to keep Havana city from growing. But planting trees in the tiniest available areas within the city itself will either interfere with the absolutely necessary urban restructuring or soon lead to more uprooting.

4. "Voluntary" mobilizations

The idea of having civil servants, students, office workers, salesgirls, stenographers, hotel clerks, barbers, and intellectuals participate in agricultural work seems an excellent one. This by and large petit-bourgeois mass has an exaggerated tendency to disdain manual labor, especially field labor and those engaged in it. (For a long time work in the Cuban canefields was done by slaves, and until 1959 many of their descendants were still treated more or less as slaves.)

However, such so-called "productive labor" must quickly become productive in practice; only mobilization of long duration meets this condition. Piecemeal work at weekends is not enough. On Sunday mornings in Havana too much time is spent waiting for the transport trucks; the sun is already high in the sky when the volunteers reach the field. If there are shade trees around the little plots of coffee that have to be harvested, it's only human to stop under them. Less useful still is night work, which is generally bad because of the absence of adequate lighting. When I noticed planting errors, broken branches, or the trunks of orange trees injured by instruments, I was often told, "It's the night work." At the Habana Libre hotel, a group that had gathered at half-past eight in the evening was still waiting for the transport truck two hours later. What condition would they be in for their regular work the next morning?

My own limited observations, and those reported to me by sympathizers of the regime, show that except in the case of *real volunteers* the productivity of these workers doesn't amount to a quarter of that of regular agricultural labor. Often it is only ten per cent, which doesn't even cover the cost of their transportation, food, and clothing. In harvesting sugarcane a good worker will cut three and a half to four tons daily, the maximum being seven tons (Stakhanovites become cardiac cases). Psychologically indoctrinated agricultural school students will cut 1·5 to 1·8 tons daily, other adolescents barely a ton; the best city dwellers 500 kilos, the others

250–300, especially if they are bureaucrats or intellectuals unused to physical effort. During the harvesting, or *zafra*, when these city dwellers spend several weeks going from place to place, they retain their regular salary, which is significantly higher than that of the agricultural workers, yet they produce a lot less. As a result, the Cuban economy is faced with high production costs allied to meager productivity, which in turn leads to privations.

True, the exodus from the rural areas had been excessive in Cuba. There was a shortage of agricultural labor even whilst young city dwellers were unemployed and becoming delinquents. There was good reason to mobilize them, and it was a good thing for white-collar workers to labor in the fields. But it would be better if they could see the results of their labor turn up on their plates. As I see it, a better solution would be to double the wages of the base agricultural workers – those who work with their hands, those who are the most deserving. In this way much of the gap between manual and intellectual work, between the city workers and the country workers, would be closed. It would take the *real* workers in the fields, or bring them back. And it could be accompanied by a general rise in the price of basic foodstuffs, which would reduce the amount of unused money and inflation, and consequently the endless queues.

5. Socialist emulation

I would rather see labor and laborers honored than the attractions of a starlet. But I couldn't help smiling when at the national head-quarters of the Committees for the Defense of the Revolution I was told about rewards for "model fathers" who regularly send their children to school on time and who participate in school meetings for the parents. We have already seen the limits of socialist emulation in the Soviet Union, where it was accompanied by high material rewards for Stakhanovites; the system seems to work better in China, where the frame of mind and the political ambiance are so different. But in Cuba I had my doubts.

A central sugar refinery wanted to win the May 1st prize by processing more cane on that day than it ever had before. It began by accumulating at the factory door wagonloads of cane that would ordinarily have been processed on April 29 and 30. The refinery broke all records and won the prize, which was celebrated with beer on May 2. Until May 4 its production rhythm was significantly slower, since the normal flow of supply wagons and trucks had been upset. What actually happened therefore was that a prize was given for a sharp drop in productivity for the April 29–May 4 period. Few of the workers were fooled; the whole thing amused them as though it were a sports match. But the Cuban economy is slowed down by these accumulated disruptions. As in China, the heavy investment brings a modest return. In 1969 only 4·3 million tons of sugar were produced as against six million in 1961.

One ministry recently declared itself a "guerilla" organization, by which was meant that it would work late into the evening without overtime pay. A canteen was organized, meals prepared, tables set, speeches made. The whole business lasted until half-past nine. Later, a little more work was done until eleven, but the fatigue the next day, when many arrived late, more than made up for the very small amount of extra work accomplished. "It looks more like a picnic than a guerilla activity," Che Guevara's sister commented sourly. Dozens of similar examples could be cited.

The cadres of the city of Camillo Cienfuegos had been mobilized for a week of *zafra*, or cane-cutting. This city is currently expanding, and the development of its industrial zone poses many problems; nevertheless the director of urban planning was also mobilized. On the last day, in the absence of most of these cadres, the local Party secretary forced a decision to prolong the mobilization for two more weeks. The urban planner had urgent work that was overdue – some Bulgarian experts were waiting for him; he asked to be released so that he could meet them but the secretary refused – maybe out of some vague notion of revenge against intellectuals. But it was a revenge allied to a total misunderstanding of the country's needs and work priorities.

6. Reasons for a firmer approach

The priority assigned to exports is understandable for at least two reasons. Cuba has a high trade deficit, especially vis-a-vis the Soviet Union, and is terribly short of convertible currency. Thus it cannot buy all the equipment it needs and is put in a position of economic and therefore political dependence on Russia. To some extent stringent rationing and the almost complete absence of most consumer goods within Cuba are also justified by the extremely high investment rate, which verges on thirty per cent – more than that in any other underdeveloped country.

But these sacrifices, which have been going on since 1961, have become unbearable for the Cubans. To what extent has a ruling group the right to impose its single-minded conception of the future – and to impose it in so disorganized a manner that the results are further aggravated? The question seems especially fair when one observes that these leaders do not themselves live in austerity (as their Chinese counterparts do). If there were true democratic participation in decision-making, one could talk of voluntary sacrifices. But this does not appear to be the case.

The organization of Cuba's economy is such that it has become all but impossible to obtain reliable data upon which to establish a more rational investment priority, leading to maximum productive growth. As I see it, this growth would necessitate making production units fiscally autonomous, establishing less arbitrary domestic and foreign price relationships, and requiring various enterprises to pay interest on the capital loaned to them. And as for agricultural production, as I have tried to point out, social and economic necessity demands the establishment of a land rent that would compensate workers for the highly variable natural (soil, climate, available water) and economic (markets, infrastructure) conditions of the land they farm.

Cuban agricultural plans are largely established in terms of physical objectives, i.e. hectares to be planted and sown. The quality of work is not given sufficient consideration. Everybody strives to work quickly – too quickly – and he tends to work badly; production costs rise in proportion to the lower yields caused by the accumulated errors. And since the solution offered by cooperative production has (unjustifiably) been rejected, nobody is directly interested in more efficient state enterprises. Though generally speaking the top administrators are well aware of their national and revolutionary responsibilities, they simultaneously satisfy their thirst for power. As for the worker who suffers under the hot sun and in badly ventilated barracks, his sufferings are increased when he receives letters from home complaining about the many difficulties of daily life. He begins to feel he's had a bellyful.

On the way to the United Nations in the summer of 1967, Alexei Kosygin stopped in Cuba. At that time it is probable that he let Fidel Castro know that the Soviet Union's "loans" to Cuba could not go on forever unlimited. The "fresh and joyous" revolution therefore had to be replaced by a firmer approach. (Castro is said to have tried to delay gas rationing by explaining to Kosygin that

Cubans couldn't do without their Sundays at the beach. Evidently no mention was made of the fact that collective buses use less gas than private autos.) The Russians therefore made clear to Castro their disillusionment with his efforts. Castro wanted good Cubans (not the *gusanos*, damn them!) to live well, but he saw that "all things he had done for them," the many free services, were possible only if they furnished a corresponding effort – which they had not. The revolution was threatened, humiliated.*

Those who had furnished Cuba with technical assistance and those who had quite generously helped to finance it were not internationalist-proletarian-philanthropists. Raul Castro had always recommended stricter discipline, discipline like the army's, the only administration that gets itself obeyed and makes things move. It was the only way to close ranks, to continue a hard, bitter, uncertain struggle. This theory interestingly illuminates the development of both the 1968 Revolutionary Offensive and the third agrarian reform. They were to lead to a general militarization of Cuba's economy.

* To avenge himself on those who had provided information to the Russians, the first thing Castro did was to launch a trial against the Escalante microfaction in the Party and disclose its links with certain members of the Soviet embassy.

5

The Price of Haste

1. A superhuman effort for ten million tons of sugar

Fidel Castro often says that when a man falls into a well neither a small, medium, nor large effort will ever get him out. The only way he can make it is by a wholly extraordinary effort. Such was the effort that he first asked and then demanded of his people so that they could climb out of the well of underdevelopment. And at the time of the April 1961 and October 1962 mobilizations, in spite of the absence from the work force of those in uniform, Cuba's production did not fail – on the contrary, it rose. This is because everybody made an exceptional effort. With these precedents in mind Castro called 1969 "the Year of Decisive Effort"; to some, this phrase meant a *last* effort, even the possibility of ultimate failure. The image has military overtones; superhuman physical efforts are often asked of guerilla fighters.

But service in a guerilla unit often lasts only a few months or years before ending with failure, death, or an exhilarating victory. The battle for Cuba's economic development is decades old, and it is far from over. Of course, posters everywhere call for "All Energies Tensed", but superhuman efforts of this kind cannot go on for decades. Castro has said that if he hadn't asked in 1964 for ten million tons of sugar by 1970, he would have got much less; this admission suggests that he hardly expected to get the ten million. The battle for ten million tons was launched in Cuban fashion by presenting the goal as a challenging sports record to be broken, "the engagement of the nation's honor." It's hard to consider it a reasonable goal.

To achieve it, part of the 1969 crop was sacrificed; in that year only 4·3 million tons, or less than half the eventual goal, was produced. This is because the central cane plantations, then in the process of expansion, were not functioning well. Not all the new equipment was in working order, nor did it always work well with older equipment. In addition the priority accorded to plantings for the "ten million-ton *zafra*" disorganized the gathering of the 1969 crop, especially in so far as transportation arrangements were concerned. In Camagüey some sugarcane was not processed until a month after it had been harvested (it is usually considered best to process it within less than twenty-four and certainly no more than forty-eight hours). Since the sugar losses in a case like that are immediate, in some cases the twelve per cent average yield extracted from the cane sank to three per cent. In terms of a national average Castro said that a little more than one per cent of sugar had been lost, since an overall eleven per cent had not been reached. (The surplus of molasses does not compensate for this.)

Part of the sugarcane that could have been processed in 1969 was credited to the 1970 crop. And the harvesting, the *zafra*, which is traditionally carried out between January and May, was officially initiated on July 14, 1969, then halted, and begun again on October 27. Then it was extended until July 1970. This is because large amounts of refined sugar from the 1969 crop had to be tipped into the vats in order to crystallize the juices from the premature 1970 crop, which had only a 5·5 per cent yield. Much of the cane had therefore been cut when it was too ripe or too green, or during the rainy period. And this also contributed to the diminished sugar yield.

Two hundred thousand tons of sugar had been produced by November 1, 1969 – in other words two per cent of the final goal. On November 6 Castro said that the seriousness of the labor shortage could be judged from the fact that the *army* had to cut between twenty and thirty per cent of the cane crop. And indeed, given the general disorder, the army seemed the best solution. But the fact that only 1150 to 1300 kilos of cut cane per day per man was foreseen showed that unenthusiastic mobilized workers were expected to predominate. Of the 200 *macheteros* who feed one loading point, often only a half-dozen or so were experienced hands.

Where have the experienced cane-cutters gone? Some are in the Ministry of the Interior because they are politically reliable. The older ones have retired, and there are few young people eager to replace them. Others have become soldiers, tractor drivers, sowers. They have been replaced by mobilized peasants and workers, by university and pre-university students, and finally by the army.

In July 1969 I thought it probable that the ten million tons of sugar were more or less potentially in the fields. But even years later there is still an urgent need to improve the coordination of harvesting and loading operations; transportation is still inadequate and maintenance is often behind schedule. There is no certainty that the refineries can be supplied on a regular basis. In the future, a high goal will be easier to achieve, for an additional 500,000 hectares of cane have been planted. Haste has caused many errors, so it should be easier to avoid them in the future. But Cuba has been making mistakes for more than ten years now, and they haven't served as much of a lesson. . . .

2. Sugarcane, bananas, and rice in Oriente province

Oriente province accounts for one-third of Cuba and can be expected ideally to furnish thirty per cent of the national sugar total. Some of its cane fields are excellent, but many others are of unequal quality, weedy, or badly situated. Acting against the advice of local peasants, the administration planted cane in zones that were so damp that the cuttings died. Semi-swampy black-clay zones were replanted three times before the attempt was given up. And all along the central road that runs through Oriente province, in the low Cauto valley, not far from these rotting cane fields, are vast plantations of bananas dying in the clay soil because of a similar lack of drainage.

As early as 1926 the first soil studies made in Cuba had concluded that these black soils were unsuitable for anything but pasture and rice paddies. They are finally being converted into paddies after many errors that could easily have been avoided by consulting the experienced agronomists on hand, or more simply by asking the peasants. Similarly, the return on many of the cane fields on the flat plains could be greatly improved by better drainage, which would raise the average per-hectare yield from thirty-five to sixty tons. The cost of this drainage would be considerably less per ton than the cane harvested with greater effort on the new plantations – especially some of those which have been established in really marginal soil. When no drainage is provided, as in the Centrale Naranjo, erosion silently opens deep crevices that interferes with mechanical weeding and harvesting. (Nowadays, the Bayamo city dweller mobilized to hoe the fields grits his teeth but retains his sense of humor: "What a lot of sugarcane there is among the weeds this year," he says to his friends as they wait in line to eat at the restaurant.)

The exciting ten million-ton goal had of course some positive aspects. Mechanized harvesting and weed-killing by herbicides are making progress, and it will soon be possible to process sugar without backbreaking hard labor. Still, if this over-ambitious goal had been delayed by a few years, the available means of production could have been more judiciously allocated. This is also true, as we shall see, in the case of winter vegetables and rice.

At the time of my visit in 1969 the Cauto valley was being transformed into a vast rice paddy that was to cover 67,000 hectares by 1970. Logically enough it was planned simultaneously to discontinue planting rice on the higher ground.

In 1966 Cuba had just about given up rice cultivation and was counting on supplying itself largely from China (where rice grows more easily than sugarcane) by means of agreements in which rice would be bartered for sugar. Given its rice shortage, Cuba, in the last stages of this agreement, was obliged to propose a rate of exchange of two pounds of sugar for one pound of rice. (This seems high to me, but it does happen that on the world market one pound of rice is worth more than two pounds of sugar.) This came after China had begun to bring political pressure to bear on Cuba to convince it of the evils of Soviet "revisionism". Spanish-language Chinese propaganda magazines were sent directly to many Cuban officials. Castro responded with two speeches, in January and March 1966, in which he energetically and legitimately defended the small nations' right to consideration.* Though Cuba's 1967 rice production had fallen to one-fourth the 1957 level, with only 31,000 hectares under cultivation, a major effort was already being planned and would have made swifter progress had it not been for the sugar priority. (I have already emphasized the high productivity of the rices developed in the Philippines. Since 1970 these rices have been almost the only ones used in Cuba for irrigated growing.)†

At the time of my arrival the Prime Minister's technical team tended to estimate production by multiplying the hectares of rice paddies in the plan by the highest per-hectare yield previously obtained. Instead of the estimated 450,000 tons (or more) that I

---

* It's too bad that he forgot this right in 1968, in relation to Czechoslovakia. It must have been because he was once again in a dependent position.

† However, southeast Asia has already abandoned IR8 for IR5, and Cuba is three years behind.

had been told of in July, the 1969 harvest was probably less than 220,000 tons of paddy rice, barely 150,000 tons of husked rice. At the December 1958 FAO conference, Rodriguez had talked of 167,000 hectares averaging 2·7 tons per hectare. In 1969 there were only 115,000 hectares, often badly cultivated, averaging two tons per hectare. So in spite of enormous investments, Cuba was still not up to the average production of paddy rice for the 1955-60 period. Fidel Castro had visited these paddies shortly before I did, and I learned that he had not seen the worst fields; yet my Cuban colleagues had not been afraid to show them to me.

The work that I saw in Puente Guillen, in the Cauto valley, had been carried out in great haste. At the time I was there only 9400 hectares out of a planned total of 40,000 hectares had been sown. Great progress was being made, but often to the detriment of quality. The ground-leveling was being done with badly adapted tools – without hydraulic lifts – and seemed unsatisfactory; it favored weed growth on the higher land and jeopardized drainage on the lower land. Some plowing had been done in over-clayed, over-humid soil. Some of the fields had been sown in unfavorable conditions and, combined with delays in spreading herbicides or fertilizers, this situation had led to a thick weed growth. The irrigation network was also being over-hastily developed; if there was a delay of several days – as happened to the south of Sancti Spiritus (Las Villas) – all the plowing tractors had to stop. Blueprints for the irrigation canals were sometimes handed out without cross-section drawings, which made one wonder if sabotage was involved.

All over Cuba the scrapers designed to clean plowing disks are mounted on overlong, overthin rods that bend when they encounter resistance. As a result the scrapers cannot function, and the disks become clogged. But Puente Guillen has no field repair shops, even though it has 135 tractors (too many, since they get in each other's way, but there's no work for them elsewhere). Even something as simple as a broken disk must go to the central workshop. The caterpillar bands on Richard tractors are too taut and have a short life. As of July 12 the fifty Richard tractors that had been delivered at the end of March had been in operation only 11,138 hours, or 222 hours per tractor. True, there had been a lot of rain, but there had been about forty "possible" days, which means that these two-man tractors worked only five and a half hours on each of those days. Disorganization and lack of enthusiasm for work seem to be the principal causes for this, but I'm not sure which of these is most responsible.

The techniques employed in Cuban rice-growing make large-scale use of aviation. Soviet Antonov-2 biplanes are used – remarkably strong planes but, I am told by Malians from the Niger Office, who have no choice but to use them, veritable gasoline hogs compared with their western equivalents. In any case the Cuban use of aircraft for agriculture is somewhat antiquated but relatively efficient. Planes sow rice, spread fertilizer and herbicides, and dust against insects and disease.

Let's get back to the ground. The men responsible for the crops are former stock farmers, *ganaderos*, who go about on horseback and refuse to give up their lassos* – symbol of their old profession, when they scorned the cane slaves bent over their hoes or machetes. They have rather too quickly been transformed into irrigationists and rice-growers: the man in charge of five hundred hectares of rice argues over the work done on "his" fields by the chief of the mechanized battalion, who is in charge of fifty large tractors and whose level of education is considerably higher. The *jef de lote* insists on quality work, but the battalion chief has to complete his plan assignment and usually carries the day, most often at the expense of good work; the other man simply doesn't carry enough weight.

3. The Camagüey "rectangle plan"

Shortly after reaching Camagüey I went to see the celebrated Majors Curbelo and Rangel, the men in charge of Cuba's largest cattle-fattening plan. The plan covered a total area of 175,000 hectares, a rectangle of about sixty by thirty kilometers, where 135,000 hectares of imported pangola pasture were being established according to a rigid blueprint. Every five kilometers a road provided access to parcels of land, each of which included four twenty-seven-hectare pastures – in other words, 108 hectares in all. In the center there was to be a shelter in which the animals would find water and troughs of sugar molasses.

To cultivate this geometric pattern, the Cubans first leveled the ground. (We will see how the Che Guevara Brigade went about

---

* It is true that big herds are still to be found in the rice plan, and when they cross the canals they ruin the banks.

clearing the area, and even now work is continuing without any previously established priority.) An attack was simultaneously made on the *marabu* thickets – so expensive to remove – to the north of the rectangle, near Nuevitas, and on the bottom-land that will have to be drained. All this in spite of the fact that the south prairies needed only to be plowed before planting pangola; elementary economic planning should have indicated plowing these fine natural pastures before setting bulldozers to work in the *marabu*. Fewer bulldozers need then have been bought, fewer debts piled up, and less haste made. . . .

But everything was leveled – all the existing hedges and enclosures – because the plan, established by the military,* had to be laid out with string, everything at right angles, rational, ideal. Provision was even made for the eventual division of each of the twenty-seven hectare parcels into four plots of a little less than seven hectares each. As I saw it, this was in no way the most economical approach. Water could be more cheaply provided if many of the rectangular plots were connected to the supply by their *short* end. The enclosure fences already there, made of wire attached to rows of small trees, not only gave the Camagüey landscape considerable charm but also offered the animals some shade. New anti-hurricane windbreak hedges were to be planted, but it would take time for them to grow. Meanwhile the tall, beautiful trees supplied a very pleasant form of shade, as well as a less expensive and more graceful shelter than the fibro-cement-roofed sheds planned. In addition, if erosion was to be avoided, the trees along the river banks would have to be spared.

"I have lots of trouble keeping the bulldozer drivers from leveling those trees as well," Curbelo told me. If a network of roads and fences had been established without disrupting what was already there, by using whatever was useful – trees and hedges – it could later have been adapted to the pre-established blueprint in successive stages; this would have required a smaller initial outlay. Besides, only time will tell if the plan is really the best one: another argument in favor of proceeding by stages. But preference is given to the guerilla habit of plunging ahead on the basis of extremely approximate information *and without worrying about costs*. This is especially true if your name is Major Curbelo and you enjoy Castro's

---

* In France the military can indulge their whims because they sponge on the national economy. In Cuba, however, they are taking over command of the national economy, and that is even more dangerous.

confidence; then you can get funds more easily and even receive your guests more handsomely. If the plan had to pay interest on re-fundable investment capital, it would be considerably more careful.

The fences that were built used enormous cement posts that seemed to be twice as thick as necessary, two meters apart and connected by five strands of barbed wire. Nobody seemed to know the cost of so expensive a fence, *and nobody cared because nobody pays.* (Luckily, only the fences along the roads have concrete posts; the others are wooden. But in the little Havana dairy farms everything is planned to be in concrete.) Smaller and more carefully manufactured posts set at four-meter intervals with a wooden slat between them to keep the wires spread would be ample.

Let's see how the pangola was being planted. Not one of the tractors was operating correctly. Many of the plow disks – made in North Korea, where the special steels are not yet well understood – were broken; others were clogged with earth and twists of wire. The cleaning scrapers either were not functioning efficiently or were completely out of order. Impassively, the major in charge looked at all the faults I pointed out, and the plowing continued, just as badly as before. I can imagine what my kulak uncle would have said if he could have seen such an operation; I can hear his insults, see him stopping the labor until everything had been fixed. He would have been especially angry with the lack of disk-cleaners.

The plan is being carried out in terms of quantity, not quality. Curbelo is a good revolutionary but is not obliged to do his job competently. He keeps a careful watch over his relations with the peasants, because that's a political problem. In the plan assigned to him there are 11,000 families who own a fourth of the livestock – 75,000 head; the other 225,000 animals belong to the state. These peasants can choose from among three possibilities: they can go along on their own, "but nobody has chosen this solution" – obviously. They can accept the plan's directives and so be assigned bulls to fatten, and some have "decided" on this. But the solution preferred by Curbelo, and the one that was therefore adopted by the great majority of peasants, is for the plan to buy all but the two or three hectares that each family keeps to grow its own food. "Our relations with the local ANAP are very good." No doubt. The next morning the leader of the Camagüey's local ANAP told me that he considers his association "a conveyor belt for feeding Party ideas to the peasants" – without evoking the equally important need, in a democratic society, for ideas to flow in the other direction as well.

The aim of the plan is to fatten bulls bought at about eight months and resold at about twenty-four months, during which time they are supposed to put on 700 grams a day, going from an average weight of 180 kilos to 425 kilos. When the pangola fields are more or less established, 500,000 young bulls are to be maintained on 135,000 hectares of pasture. This figure is expected to rise rather quickly to *a million head*, or 800 per 108-hectare unit, by 1980. There will also be a more intensive cultivation of napier grass. All this is reasonable if work could be done more efficiently, if all the details could be organized correctly. Given the present atmosphere, I wouldn't want to be responsible for a million head, but the prospect doesn't seem to worry Major Curbelo, nor does the bad plowing. This absence of concern is what worries me most.

4. The Camagüey "triangle" dairy plan

The gently undulating plateau that surrounds the city of Camagüey and includes areas where sugarcane is raised was once used for extensive stock farming. In 1960 I visited a 6000-hectare operation for fattening 6000 young bulls. It made do with about ten permanent employees and about a hundred temporary workers during October to machete the constantly regrowing underbrush. At about the beginning of the century guinea grass had been planted there because the return on it is higher than with natural pastures; but the intensification here didn't go very far. The extreme underutilization of men and soil that characterized most Cuban agriculture in 1958 "called for" a revolution.

Castro's dairy plan for this region will constitute considerable progress. It will first accumulate 746,000,000 cubic meters of water in thirteen large and about a hundred small reservoirs. Here too pangola pastures will be established, for pangola is more productive than guinea grass, especially if fertilizer and irrigation are employed. The area will be subdivided into parcels of eighty-five hectares for the cows, 1·70 hectares for heifers, and 3·4 hectares for somewhat older animals. Such a subdivision strikes me as almost lunatic in view of its cost. The plan will embrace a total of 470,000 hectares, of which 360,000 will be agricultural. Since most of the plots will be for cows, this means more than 250,000 fenced-in tiny pastures (each one an average 1·44 hectares, 120 by 120 meters).

Such a pattern represents a fence length – taking into account roadside borders and the paths to milking sheds – *of more than 60,000 kilometers*, one and a half times the circumference of the earth! If the same density were to be adopted for the 3·2 million hectares of pasture that Cuba is supposed to have by 1980, this would mean 530,000 kilometers of fences! If a thick concrete post weighing fifty kilos were placed not every two meters but every four meters, 132 million posts would be required. Since they each weigh fifty kilos, that means 6·5 million tons of concrete, or more than a million tons of cement. I don't know if the Central Planning Committee has worked these figures out. Luckily it will never come to this; but it is time to see if the posts need be so thick and so closely planted.

Greater economy could be realized if Fidel Castro had not decided (somewhat hastily, as usual) that electrified fencing would be impractical. He told me that its use would "lead to chaos," although the workers at the Indio Hatuey fodder research station, in Matanzas province, learned to make *good* use of it in only a few days. Electrified fencing would permit parcels about ten times as large and a proportionate additional reduction in fencing cost. Such savings would make the cost of the electrical equipment seem ridiculously low.

But that isn't its only advantage. The small 57-are parcels in the little dairies near Havana were grazed clean in four days during the heavy summer growth. The first two days the cows ate the higher grass, which is over-rich in proteins; the last two days they ate the lower growths, which have a heavier fiber content. Their ration was therefore constantly unbalanced, and to make sure that they received enough nitrogen, a pound of concentrate for every liter of milk produced was necessary. For the most part this concentrate has to be imported; when the Russians ship it from Canada, this means an expenditure of convertible currency for the socialist camp.

But if the cows were to eat the entire length of the plant every day, they would not, given the milk return established for the great majority of F1 crossbreeds, need concentrates; instead one could, and should, add molasses. An entire series of economies could be achieved in this way. That is, if here, as in the brigade of the Camille Cienfuegos fertilizer plant, the team was formed as the work went along, and all *a priori* notions were rejected, even if they came from Castro; but this is something that is becoming harder and harder to do!

The plan provides for nourishing three cows per hectare, which is possible with well-established pastures. Projections call for further intensification: for maintaining, by 1980, 1·4 million cows, about

840,000 of which would be in lactation every day, and for producing
8·4 million liters of milk – or a liter a day for every Cuban. If a little
less than 300,000 hectares are devoted to cows, that would make
five cows per hectare, which is clearly excessive. The sharp division
between the two plans for milk and for meat is not always justified.
The best possible use of guinea grass is for meat production. On
black clay lands, or on those rich in calcium, or those on a slope,
guinea grass is so solidly established that it's best to keep it; besides,
it quickly outgrows the pangola variety when attempts are made to
establish the latter. The guinea grass could be reserved for the
fattening of non-productive cows, or for grown cattle.

Finally, the milk and meat plans each relegate to one of two small
corners, far from the center, the space for crops for human consumption: tubers and bananas. Nobody said anything to me about
fruit or vegetable gardens. Some day consideration should be given
to a better food supply for workers; this would only be normal for a
regime that calls itself socialist.

5. Communism can only lead to victory: the Isle of Youth

It was called the Isle of Pines, off the southern coast of Havana
province. It was said that pirates had stayed there, that there was
buried treasure. . . . The pre-revolutionary government had built a
prison there, and in 1959 the island had only 13,000 inhabitants and
11,000 cattle. Of the 500 hectares being farmed, 400 were planted
with grapefruit, especially in the alluvial stretches of bottom land.
The Isle of Youth – its present name – is now approaching a population of 40,000, and plans call for a rise to 125,000. In 1969 it
already had 70,000 cattle, and had plans for 240,000, with a daily
production of a million liters of milk. In line with this, work was
being done to establish 110,000 hectares of improved pasture land
and to accumulate nearly a half billion cubic meters of water. There
is hope that citrus fruits will make the island's fortune, but the dams
have flooded the most valuable bottom lands.

When I arrived at the airport of this Isle of Youth* the first poster

---

* I was to visit the Isle of Youth on Monday, July 21, at half past four in
the morning. I was ready to leave for the airport, but there had been a counter-
order, apparently linked to the fact that my rather critical general report had
been turned over to Fidel Castro by the Rector a few hours before. I did not
leave until forty-eight hours later and was no doubt preceded by instructions on
how to receive me.

I saw proclaimed: "We want to transform nature." The second added "and society." What troubled me was that the second poster showed a helmeted soldier towering over the young man and woman on each side of him. It is becoming clearer and clearer that it is the army that is charged with transforming Cuban society.

Major Mir, who "governs" the island, explained: "A human being has two essential characteristics: his intelligence and his emotions. Devotion to the community will be the fundamental basis for the creation of wealth. A man *makes himself* through work even as he does this work. Our Party, our people, want us to change this island into a sort of paradise." After emphasizing that vagabonds and lazy people were not admitted to the island, he somewhat abruptly and awkwardly – his level of education, he said, was not very high – concluded: "Besides, communism can only lead to victory." It was as though he had been forced into this position. This is precisely Fidel Castro's situation, and explains his attitudes.

Let's look into the "paradise" at the southern end of the island and examine one of the three cattle-breeding bases, Number 1, known as Réforma. It covers 36,000 hectares (one-sixth of the island), 14,700 of which have been planted with pangola, 510 with napier; the remainder, about 21,000 hectares, is still natural pasture whose yield is unquestionably less than a quarter than that of the artificially created pastures. These pastures have been rather badly established – the pangola grass is not often dominant – and the work was done too quickly, probably in the same way as that at the rectangle. This impression was quickly confirmed by the present density of the livestock herd: 23,000 cattle of all ages, the great majority young, and less than 11,000 full-grown. That corresponds to less than one small adult bovine per hectare of artificial pasture, if the natural pastures provide a density of only a fourth of the pangola pasture.

This figure contrasts sharply with the ten heads announced by Castro at the Niña Bonita Genetic Center, or even the five cows per hectare promised by the triangle plan or elsewhere – notably in a small dairy farm on the Carretera Centrale, east of Havana. (This farm was also named Niña Bonita, and 288 cows lived there on fifty-four hectares, half excellent pangola, half napier grass and lucerne.) The large-scale projects never achieve the yields of the first small enterprises that can be more carefully tended. And the gap between them makes one wonder about the outlook for 1980 for Camagüey and for Cuba itself. Of all the figures I passed on to Castro, it was this meager density that struck him most – so much so that he was sure that I was mistaken. For he is not always correctly informed by his own people, who are somewhat wary of his outbursts. This means that he is at the mercy of his enthusiasms and encouraged to make faulty decisions.

The Réforma base had 550 so-called permanent workers. Actually, ninety-five per cent were men who had been assigned to work there for periods of between six weeks and two years. In addition to this there were 545 soldiers – apprentice peasants – whose productivity was *not half* that of the workers. 550 workers, not counting the soldiers, for 23,000 animals, when scarcely 500 liters of milk are produced daily, means a very low work productivity, even bearing in mind the installations and the fact that milking is done by hand.

A small dairy farm belonging to the base has ninety F1 milch cows which in July 1969 were producing 836 liters of milk daily. Seven permanent workers took care of them with the help of eighteen soldiers split into two groups of nine, the first group on duty from one to nine o'clock in the morning; the second from two to nine o'clock in the evening. If the eighteen soldiers are considered the equivalent of seven workers, that would mean fourteen workers for ninety cows, more than double the proportion in the small private dairies near Havana (which have comparable milk yields). A modern dairy in the United States would need only one and a half workers; true, there would be a lot more equipment, but also a lot more milk.*

I quickly saw that the soldiers' enthusiasm for their work was like that of a private sweeping up in the company area – I was once one myself. The workers were somewhat better, but their attitude was that of a very average civil servant and they won't break any records. "We do what we're paid to do," one of them said to a friend who visited the island shortly before me. I searched in vain for some visible sign of that famous revolutionary conscience. Even at the kindergarten on the Réforma base, fourteen women were taking care of thirty-five children, which is overdoing things; at the same time other women were assigned to very hard work.†

The foreign visitor is astonished to see more workers involved in clean-up work than in milking the cows. Everywhere else in the

* "It is certain that capitalism had attained high levels of organization, efficiency and productivity that declined after the revolution." Armando Hart, *Juventad Rebel*, November 2, 1969.

† In 1969 there were in Cuba 364 of these *circulos infantils* taking good care of 44,000 children. The general employee density is less than in this case, but often seems high.

world the opposite is true. But the military like things to be clean. Still, the endless clean-up of the cattle's shade shelters is absurd. There's no reason why the dung can't accumulate and just be raked together from time to time. Another and bigger surprise: the clean-up waters, heavy with dung and urine, are dumped into the stream, which they then pollute. Nobody thinks of retaining them for their fertilizer value.* Therefore even more currency has to be used for the purchase of fertilizers, but it's not the officials who pay.

Sometimes plans are made to install septic ditches near the barns, like those used for houses. The medical corps has evidently made itself forcefully felt in the agronomic domain (the plan's research and conception has been confided to the Rector of the University of Havana who, like his assistants, is a doctor). This arrangement would result in less pollution, but the fertilizer loss would continue. In my discussions with them I felt as if I no longer spoke the same language as my Cuban colleagues – soldiers or doctors. For them everything appeared so simple. Things are more complex to the agronomist, especially if he's concerned about costs.

After the stock farms I was shown the Isle of Youth's grapefruit orchards, established before the revolution. After insisting on seeing the new planting operations, I learned that of the 13,400 hectares to be planted by 1969, only 1045 had been planted. On that day, July 23, three hectares were planted (forty hectares had been planted the day before), but everybody agreed that spring is the best time to plant successfully.

At midday thousands of plants were lying in the full sun alongside the holes dug for them; they were not to be set into the ground until the next day. With their roots in polyethylene bags of compost they would not die, but they would feel the effects. A rational plan would have been to distribute in the evening or very early morning only those plants that were to be set in the same day. And it would have been better if the planting had taken place during the morning, but it began later and went on until 5 in the evening. Accompanied by the man in charge of planting I looked in vain from half-past three until five for a crew still at work. We found one at three minutes past five, just as they had stopped. The young women

---

* The United States and Sweden, wealthy countries where labor is more expensive than elsewhere, carefully collect this organic material, for it ensures a good amount of humus and continuing fertility. Cuba doesn't know about humus and scorns manure.

planters had been given no training, and fertilizer had been thrown any which way around the holes. And yet this sort of thing can be quickly learned.

The effects of erosion on the sandy slopes were to be seen immediately after the first rainfalls. I asked the man in charge why the planting did not follow the contour lines. He flushed and became embarrassed and finally said that this approach had been proposed to Commandante Castro, who had rejected it. He's the one to decide everything, even down to the details. True, just as with the electric fences, the issue is debatable: tractor work would be more complicated with contour planting, but whenever there's doubt the best thing is to experiment instead of making an *a priori* decision, so that results could be compared, at least on a small scale.

The 1968 plantings along the island's western route seemed in very sad shape. Just about everything needed to be redone. Some suffered from too much water, caused by the later creation of reservoirs. This should have been foreseen. Drainage is required in the bottom land and had been too long in coming; the trees were turning yellow. Since the bottom lands, where the best results might have been expected, were flooded, planting had also been done in the gravelly soil near the Citrus Fruit School – thin, over-dry soil that could not be irrigated and from which one can expect little. Even the trees on the slopes were hardly in good shape. Many had been dug up, and those that were left had broken branches and bruised trunks. The lack of care was obvious everywhere, and too many workers didn't give a damn. North of Ciégo de Avila, aspersion watering of the new citrus plantings is badly organized: water is wasted and the watering is done only irregularly.* Such extensive plantings call for a maximum amount of technical skill, and it must be speedily acquired, especially in the absence of material incentive. Of course many orchards, such as those I saw at Jaguey Grande, south of Mantanzas, have been made under better conditions – although even there the auger used to make the planting holes was often too small (sixty centimeters) and attempts were made to plant in too rocky soils.

In 1969 Cuba's citrus plan called for planting a fantastic total of 270,000 hectares by 1975. If it were to succeed it would make Cuba the world's leading exporter of citrus fruits, with five million tons

---

* Aspersion watering is illegal in California, where it was found to encourage the growth of fungus diseases.

sold annually after 1985. An investment of such magnitude absolutely cannot endure mediocrity; it requires good sense, initiative at
the base; wide technical knowledge; and deep well-aerated, well-
drained soils. But the documentary material assembled in Cuba on
this problem is not very up-to-date; there's nothing in it about the
most modern techniques or about the struggle to combat erosion. I
suggested therefore that they consult an international expert in the
field who, if he were heeded, could cut down expenses and raise
income by tens of millions of dollars.* This had already been done,
in a less important agricultural matter, with Claude Py and the
translation of his book on pineapples.

6. La Sierra de Rosario

Officials in Cuba are not sufficiently concerned about the problem
of soil erosion, especially on the moderate slopes of the plains –
where the rains of June 1969 had underlined the importance of the
matter. It was nevertheless decided to prepare to cultivate the steeper
slopes, after having (logically enough) brought the plains under
cultivation first. In line with this an anti-erosion experiment was
begun, east of Cayajabos, on the western part of the Sierra de los
Organos, Pinar del Río province. I have pointedly called it an
experiment and not a systematic experimentation. For only a single
method has been planned for forests and savannahs: the use of very
large parallel terraces on contour lines.

The experiment started with the basic idea to "dominate" the
mountain. I would have preferred an attempt to study nature and
see how, *by adapting to it*, one could make maximum use of its
resources and potentialities. No, in this military society man commands, dominates, *violates* nature. Enormous bulldozers therefore
carved out terraces a good four meters wide along the slope,
separated by vertical drops of about ten meters. About 160 kilometers of these terraces had already been completed without anybody having an idea as to *what they cost*. I suggested the possibility
of smaller and less widely spaced terraces, such as are found in
North Africa, which displace a smaller volume of earth and cost
much less to build. Captain Osmani Cienfuegos, brother of the late
Camillo Cienfuegos, told me that it would be mechanically impossible, but in fact it would actually have been easier (for example, by

---

* A Cuban specialist spent two weeks in the Israeli orange groves; hardly a
very long time.

simply supplying their Richard 180-HP tractors with angle-dozers). Certainly several different formulae could have been tried. But no – the concern was to perfect a single formula that once again had been selected *a priori*.

On the terraces hard-wood mahogany trees that will not grow well in isolation are being planted. They are interspersed with coffee plants in both forest soils and savannah soils. In the latter the coffee yields may be very low and not economical – especially since the dispersion of the trees increases the necessary displacements for their care and for the harvesting. Perhaps some other crop would be more suitable? Every time I talk of economy I seemed to be asking foolish questions. Coffee had been decided on everywhere since the plan was a coffee-mahogany plan and that's all there was to it. A decision handed down from above is never questioned on the site; it is put into action more or less well, with more or less difficulty. And yet this was a *pilot project*!

In places the slope is gentler, and a solid coppice efficiently holds the earth. This would have made it possible to plant mahogany trees by simply clearing the lines on which they were to be planted, and no terrace would have been necessary. But that would have been *less spectacular*.

7. Early vegetables

A Mr Brambilla, an agent of Les Halles Paris, went to Fidel Castro himself and offered to buy ten to fifteen million dollars' worth of early vegetables. Castro accepted, and he was right to do so because it would be to Cuba's advantage: western Europe annually consumes 50,000 tons of early winter vegetables (sweet peppers and, especially, tomatoes) over and above its own production. The agreement reached with Brambilla in 1968 called for Cuba to deliver during the five months December–April 5000 tons of early vegetables in 1969, 20,000 to 25,000 tons in 1970, and 40,000 to 50,000 tons in 1971 – as well as a significant amount of other products.

With pimentos at $400 a ton and tomatoes at $300 a ton (FOB Havana), the figure for 1969 in no way represented a top limit, since the West German market and many others were also interested. North Africa doesn't begin heavy production until the beginning of May and southern Europe only shortly after that. At sixty tons of tomatoes per hectare it would need only 1500 to 2000 hectares – allowing for non-exportable qualities – to reach this production with

3000 *careful* men. A French horticultural technician whom I had seen at work in Pointe Noire in the Congo, Mr Amadieu, was placed at Cuba's disposal after March 1969, and recent hybrid seeds of tomatoes, cucumbers, and pimentos were shipped to Cuba.

The seeds were never sown. Amadieu had a great deal of trouble finding them, and by the time he did the tomato seeds were already spoiled. The Agronomical Institute of Catalina, in Güines, at the western end of Cuba, had been unable to organize a real effort. That winter only 1200 tons were exported, a fourth of what had been planned. In the summer of 1969 there seemed to be no possibility that more than 5000 tons would be exported during the winter of 1970, only twenty per cent of what had been contracted for.

In Cuba the exportation of a single case of vegetables involves packing, sorting, and refrigeration, as well as loading and export authorizations; this requires the coordination of thirteen government bureaux. None of them is in a hurry. The anti-bureaucratic struggle of the Cuban revolution has not been very vigorous, and certainly not very successful. At every stage there was a glaring lack of concern.

Let's take a look at the situation in the fields. Careless harvesting made for a high proportion of bruised tomatoes and pimentos. Many of the plants were picked while too unripe: the peppers were wrinkled, the tomatoes were green, and the whole lot unsaleable. Excessive watering too close to harvest time had endangered the conservation of the vegetables, as did over-rough handling and transportation: the sorter-calibrator shook them "as though they were potatoes." Sorting is also sometimes done by schoolchildren, who don't know how to do the job correctly, or by women who are too frequently replaced. Yet these vegetables are delicate de luxe products whose appearance is important, and they had to survive a long trip. Not all the Cubans involved cared. On one truck already loaded with fifty cases of eggplants the workers heaped three tons of pineapples: forty-seven cases were spoiled.

I emphasized to President Dorticós the importance of a contract such as the one from Les Halles to the Cuban economy; it would enable Cuba to pay off a large part of her commercial deficit with France* and thus to continue equipment purchases:

---

* In 1968, France's exports to Cuba totaled 275 million francs, and its imports from Cuba 73 million francs. The Brambilla project could have supplied Cuba with 90 million francs in 1971 – in other words, forty-five per cent of the 1968 commercial deficit.

tractors, trucks, public-works machinery, etc. Dorticós said that Cuba could no doubt manage to sow and cultivate the promised vegetables under the present systems for mobilizing workers; later, however, given the paucity of labor all might be lost as a result of insect attacks, diseases not treated in time, or harvesting by non-qualified help. It is unfortunate that the disorganization has reached such proportions that 3000 workers cannot be assigned for six consecutive months to a task capable of bringing in so much revenue. To earn as many dollars with sugar would require much more labor and vastly more equipment. If the interests of the workers were engaged we'd see results. But the dogmatism of Cuba's leaders is opposed to this: the leaders suffer from little privation. In any case in July 1969 Dorticós felt that the contract would be honored at the expense of the tobacco crop, for which the market was assured. But until this time tobacco has largely been grown by small farmers. What can become of it when attempts are everywhere being made to eliminate the peasantry?

8. The militarization of education and of the labor force

It would be unworthy to criticize the haste with which in 1961 Cuba struggled to eliminate illiteracy: this campaign was one of the revolutionary regime's most handsome successes. As a result, elementary education developed rapidly, but this haste made adequate teacher training very nearly impossible. Because of this, Cuban elementary education today is in bad shape, and the level of both secondary and university education has gone down.

In 1968–9 there were 1·45 million elementary students and 174,000 secondary students; these figures represent enormous progress over the Batista era. However, 2·2 million Cubans were between the ages of six and sixteen, which means that almost half a million were not attending school. In addition there are an estimated 137,000 "dropouts." (Enormous posters everywhere call on them to return to school.) Finally, 700,000 pupils are more than two years behind their grade level.

To improve this situation a semi-boarding system was developed; pupils were encouraged to stay in school with a midday meal. (The professors too are semi-boarders.) This has greatly relieved working parents, especially in view of rationing. It was thus possible during the first cycle of secondary education to orient pupils toward the technical subjects which constitute the whole of the second cycle –

thereby tolling the bell for the humanities! This technological education was under the control of a vice-minister of the Armed Forces
Ministry. Military training was therefore given at all levels. By the
time they're eight young girl pupils march in step – which irritates
old radicals like Daniel Gúerin or me, since we have not forgotten
some of socialism's libertarian and anti-militaristic traditions.

If this education isn't working as well as it might, it is first of all
because of the dogmatic refusal to use the majority of pre-revolutionary teachers, even for technical subjects, unless they are unconditional revolutionists. Beginning from nothing, a hasty attempt
has been made to train available personnel, but their aptitude for
the job varies sharply and is often very low. And secondary education
is too often a mere adjustment of deficiencies at the elementary level.
The first part of secondary education is still a general one, but no
doubt not for long, since it will probably follow the trend of later
secondary education, which in Cuba is called "pre-university" and
was recently attached to the revolutionary armed forces. The young
are mobilized between the ages of fifteen to twenty-seven, during
which time they may not leave Cuba. In this education military
combat training accounts for an entire day each week. These
students contributed fifteen days to the *zafra* in 1967, forty-five
days in 1968, and four months in 1969; in 1970 the period was
undoubtedly longer!

Because of the lack of teachers, part of the curriculum is taught
by older students who more or less inadequately transmit what they
themselves have inadequately learned. The result is undigested
lessons given by immature teachers without professional experience
or training. The education is hyperspecialized; teachers who deal
with a limited subject and know nothing of related fields – who are
themselves the product of a mediocre general education – can only
give their students a kind of gloss, not real training. For example, Mr
Caty, a French agronomist who was sent to Cuba by UNESCO,
noted serious gaps in the way his subject was taught: professors at
the Institute of Technology didn't know the names of the most
common plants or their requirements, which is even more serious
(acid or alkaline soils, well-drained soils or not, poor or fertile
soil . . .). Soil laterization is also unknown, though it is a serious
menace to the future of this country, especially in Oriente province
and on the Isle of Youth where the dry periods are accentuated. (If
these soils are disturbed too much this menace, which is totally un-
familiar to the Cubans, is accelerated. Though the threat is not as

serious as it is in Africa, it is far from absent. Natural fertilizer would inhibit laterization, but old agronomists are not listened to.)

One provincial official had promised a secondary boarding school funds and equipment if ninety-five per cent of the students passed their exams. The teachers were alerted: marks had to be given with this in mind. Only the English teacher, a foreigner, handed in reports of student performances at unsatisfactory levels, saying that only one per cent could pass. "It wasn't a suggestion, but an order," replied the director. The teacher therefore prepared the official answers and gave the students corrected copies to study. The next day the exam was given officially; one per cent failed. Given this success, the Maxim Gorki Institute, which recruits future teachers, thought that it might find many worthwhile candidates at the school but selected, in fact, only one. Ninety per cent of the students chose to serve in the navy, and the official investigator was somewhat surprised, since Cubans usually don't like the sea. "It's the only service in which you can travel," replied one student. (We should note here the great progress made in Cuba's merchant marine and fishing fleet. Many of the boats sail under the Russian flag or have Russians in the crew.)

At the end of October 1969, at a meeting of sugarcane technicians in Camagüey, Armando Hart, a member of the political bureau, gave a speech the essential points of which I might usefully summarize here. These young people were going to serve as a base for all technical, educational, ideological, and *political* work, he said, as a springboard for enhanced effort, because they were an enthusiastic group, *politicized*, formed by the revolution itself. From June to August, he emphasized, the weeding of the cane fields mobilized 100,000 to 120,000 workers, and this meant enormous disorder for industry, construction, transportation, and other vital sectors of the Cuban economy – on behalf of a kind of work that was typical not even of capitalism but of a slave society. In Camagüey a complete weeding of the cane fields had never been carried out; 13,000 hectares were lost because of the rains. Herbicides would make it possible to weed with 7000 to 8000 men, but very few young people had entered the Sugarcane Institute that year and only twenty-four had completed the course; urban young people had no inclination for this kind of work. This kind of argument was inadmissable, unacceptable; the young people and the Party had to undertake a more intense political task of propaganda and persuasion.

That year another 3000 to 4000 workers left the countryside for jobs in the city; it was a veritable hemorrhage. Their wages bore almost no relationship to the quantity of goods they could buy. Once these workers had dispersed, they could not be reorganized. Socialism, Hart therefore emphasized, necessarily imposes the concentration of workers in encampments. (I'd rather say that it requires their mobilization.) He pointed out that the encampments offer enormous possibilities for political work and the struggle to raise productivity.

The revolution, he added, broke up the wage mechanism (it's evidently easier to organize and direct a society of slaves). Workers now had *moral* reasons to increase production. But, he noted, the necessary application of modern techniques was incompatible with technical indiscipline and ignorance. (When he called for "doing things on a large scale, and quickly, very quickly, explosively" I was reminded of the Chinese Great Leap Forward in 1958, which didn't work too well; he acknowledged that it was very difficult.) But "if all the labor force was in encampments, like the Columna, ah, then we suppose *ideal* conditions, it is *toward this* that we must work." It was quite clear: the development of the Cuban economy could be accelerated by the militarization of the labor force. (But the examples of militarization that we have already seen and those we will study later are scarcely encouraging.)

Finally, Hart remarked that Cuba had achieved the highest degree of socialization of the means of production in the entire world, because cooperative property, rural private property, and many other capitalistic residues still exist in other socialist countries. Here for the first time a top leader publicly admitted that the total elimination of private property in Cuba was the official objective of the revolutionary leadership. In July 1969 a great deal of caution had been taken in explaining to me the voluntary nature of this trend, the retention of private crops for family subsistence, the beautiful furnished houses offered in compensation, etc. Did this speech mean that the last "privileges," if I may call them that, would in turn disappear?

9. How much progress?

I do not pretend that this chapter gives a fully representative picture of the Cuban situation at the end of the 1960s, which would in any event be very difficult for a foreigner to evaluate fairly. Production statistics are not published, and most of what is available concerns areas under cultivation. Everywhere there are signs of heavy investment, of the rapid formation of technical cadres, but their value seems to vary considerably and is on the average inadequate. Still, one way or another the Cuban economy is making progress. Castro judiciously emphasized hydraulic engineering; artificial insemination is increasing the number of heifers; pangola grass is extending its rich domain; heavy-yield rices have finally been sown, albeit too late, and plantings are spreading quickly, even if not under the best conditions.

The official culprit for admitted errors is well known; its name is underdevelopment. This makes it possible to cover up incompetence, inertia, paralysis of individual initiative, conformism, gigantism, waste, and disorganization. In reacting to these weaknesses militarization adds to previous errors the faults of an authoritarian regime: rigidity of conception, lack of nuance and adaptation to circumstances, elimination of exchange of opinion, and passivity in execution.

The blockade and the alleged threat of invasion enable the regime to justify the privations imposed on the population. The blockade is a hindrance, of course, but the port of Havana is nevertheless full of ships (which due to the general disorganization of the port usually have to wait too long to be unloaded).* The militarization of the economy, especially in agriculture, is creating a structure that can offer rare advantages, but it is proving difficult to manage efficiently at the present stage of development. This will be even more true if for the first time in history the important factor of material incentives is rejected in such a large-scale experiment.† The time has come to look more closely at this military society that is unique in the world.

---

* It is morally indefensible to prohibit ships of companies dealing with Cuba from docking in the United States. Cuba has committed no act of war against the United States, although America has done so against Cuba.

† The precedents – convents, kibbutzim, or phalansteries – were or are only microcosms. China's similar efforts were made in a totally different political ambiance.

6

Communism, a Military Society or Personal Power?

1. A unique militarized agriculture

A lot of work and discipline are necessary to build socialism, especially if a country's initial economic level is low. As soon as mankind emerges from primitive or patriarchal societies, other motivations must be found if the formidable profit motive – man's most powerful incentive to activity – is rejected. From Sudan to Libya, in Peru if not in Mali and Bolivia, the military are showing that they can be the ferment for a more or less progressive evolution in the Third World. This simultaneously nationalist and populist evolution, once it recognizes the obstacles and contradictions that can make it aware of its limits, could one day lead to socialism.

As far as agriculture is concerned, the Cuban revolutionary government's first step had been to eliminate a capitalistic agricultural system that had many faults (under-utilization of both men and land) but was fairly efficient. The socialist agriculture that followed – with the cooperatives and *granjas* – mobilized available resources and equipped and over-equipped itself, but it was unable to re-establish efficiency. Its failure was implicitly acknowledged by the present reorientation, that of the special plans, which we shall examine now. It is within the framework of the revolutionary offensive that we can see the outline for the militarization of the entire Cuban economy.

Cuban agriculture is certainly more and more militarized. From the beginnings of the agrarian reform, the army has played an essential role, and agriculture is now directed from a national command post – *puesto de mando*. All important jobs are entrusted to the army; all important enterprises are headed by a major, a captain, or a first lieutenant. Major Parra would have liked me to share his enthusiasm for the immense relief map of Cuba that, when I was there, was soon to be installed in the command post: all the agricultural plans are represented on the map, with separate lighting circuits that make it possible to instantly illuminate, say, all rice paddies, all citrus orchards, all grazing pastures, etc. Now indeed this should greatly impress many foreign visitors – that is indeed perhaps one of its primary purposes. The mere existence of this map will tend to encourage the idea that Cuba's present allocation of crops has achieved a kind of perfection.

Similar *puestos de mando* have been or will be established on provincial, regional, and plan levels, and all agriculture will in a sense be codified. Each command post is beginning to receive from its production units certain daily, weekly, and monthly reports, transmitted by telephone, teletype, radio,* telegraph, and messenger. There is much genuine concern to establish exactly what kind of information is necessary at each level, how often it should be supplied, and by what means it should be transmitted. But the problem is not easy, for if information is over-stressed the production unit cadres will be swamped by paperwork (as are the *granja* cadres); on the other hand, if the command center does not have sufficient data, its decisions may not be relevant to the actual situation. As I watched my Cuban friends discussing this question, I sought for a solution that would tend toward more decentralization, more initiative, more autonomy, and, therefore, more responsibility at the base. I caught myself just as I was about to suggest self-management of base units, but this would have exposed me to accusations of Yugoslav heresy.

This military structure – and its essential nature is military – does not place enough confidence in the base. Too many things are decided on paper by those in charge, so that the workers, who have been mobilized and organized into brigades, simply carry out orders as though they were soldiers. The supervisor of one sector of a rice plantation (the non-com) receives orders covering everything that he is to do day by day, from the day the rice grain sown germinates to 110 or 120 days later – the date established for its harvesting and threshing.

* The leaders of the plans or large administrative bodies have a transmitter-receiver radio in their jeeps so that during inspection tours they can be in constant communication with their headquarters and in a position to make urgent decisions. These radios were formerly used by Batista's police, and they make it possible to accustom cadres to the use of radio for military purposes. The radios can be used in situations of internal and external security (parachute attacks, landings, etc.). Their transmissions are no doubt picked up by US radio spy ships.

4

Cuban agriculture, however, is charged with a complex of tasks infinitely more complicated than those carried out by a peacetime army. Centralization does of course have certain advantages: it permits the immediate imposition of innovations on a nationwide basis without having to win over the adherence of the peasants, not all of whom are sufficiently educated to understand the anticipated benefits. The amount of fertilizer, the kinds of equipment, and the cultivation techniques to be used are all questions determined at the "technocratic" level, which is supposed to be well informed about the most modern methods.

But we have already examined many of the on-the-spot difficulties, and we will come across others. For example, the soldiers in charge of work teams carry revolvers, which is understandable (the threat of sabotage) but it makes me uneasy. (I have elsewhere noted that in Central and South America the man in charge – either the owner or a manager – can be spotted by the fact that he carries a revolver, whereas his workers have machetes.) As a symbol of power this is not very appealing.

2. An agricultural drill field: the Che Guevara Brigade

The rehearsal for the army's takeover seems to have begun in October 1967, when the Che Guevara Brigade went to work, a brigade composed of thirty-six heavy equipment platoons, each comprising 117 men and twenty heavy tractors and bulldozers.* It was intended to reclaim tens of thousands of hectares of land for planting sugarcane, rice, or pangola. About a thousand caterpillar tractors, bulldozers, and tanks assembled on the Cauto plain; the mechanized troops, passed in review by Castro himself, were given the take-off signal. The brigade was supposed to "cut to pieces" its new enemy – nature – and it was real warfare, right down to field communiqués. After reaching Camagüey, however, the brigade

---

* Michel Gutelman has pointed out that all workers, tractor drivers, or officers of the Che Guevara Brigade earn the same pay, 160 pesos a month, plus food and board. This makes them privileged people in comparison with the ordinary workers of the *granjas* or the Plans, who earn between 85 and 120 pesos a month and generally have to pay for their canteen meals. For that matter, the Brigade's egalitarianism does not even prevail in the army, where there are generally three separate messes: one for officers, one for non-coms and professional soldiers, and a third for temporary recruits, who are not often enthusiastic about the food, especially after hearing the stories told by friends who serve in the officers' mess.

broke up into small groups and there was less talk of it. By April 1968 it reached Las Villas, but the column had stretched out considerably and the rearguard was still in Cauto. In 1969 there was occasional news that a given plan had been aided by elements of the brigade. Finally it was disbanded and absorbed into a special mechanized army section used in agricultural work which in June 1969 took over the management of the country's hydraulic resources.

In clearing the land, then, the brigade followed a line of march roughly paralleling that of the rebel columns ten years earlier – a guerilla-inspired, sentimental criterion for work that did not adequately take economic considerations into account. (I have already pointed out how the plans for improved pastures in Camagüey were carried out by clearing all the land simultaneously instead of systematically beginning in areas where it could be seen that the investment outlay would bring the greatest return.) More seriously, the clearing methods could hardly have been more brutal. In uprooting trees the crews scooped up goodly amounts of topsoil rich in humus and shoved it, along with the tree trunks, into piles that were then set on fire. Behind the noble platoons of bulldozers came the modest foot soldiers, the forestry people, laborers who with their little axes spent endless hours chopping up wood to be used for posts, sawmills, or fuel. If one less bulldozer had been bought – so many are under-utilized that it would have been enough to organize the work better and speed up the repairs – the money thus saved could have been used to buy hundreds of power saws, with which one man could do the work of fifty. Giving priority to the heaviest equipment does not necessarily ensure the acquisition of the most economical or most productive equipment. Until now this consideration seems to have been ignored in Cuba.

As I have said, brutal land clearing such as we have seen in Camagüey destroys trees that could otherwise have been used for shade, for protecting river banks against erosion, for posts, for anti-hurricane protection. (Anti-hurricane hedges will soon crisscross the country, but it takes a matter of years for them to be planted and to grow high enough.) Yet the fear of hurricanes haunts Castro, especially since Hurricane Flora in October 1963, which flooded all the Oriente plains and in which he and a rescue crew were almost killed. Erosion worries him less: indiscriminate land clearing encourages erosion on every moderate slope, and yet no adequate measures have been taken to arrest it. The new irrigation reservoirs won't fill with mud for twenty-five years, but if their feeders were better protected and if the plowing of steep hills was prohibited their usefulness could be greatly extended. This would seem more sensible than building monumental terraces in Pinar del Rio.

To achieve erosion protection the Sierra Maestra peasants – who do after all have to go on living – would need land on more gentle slopes in exchange for that on the steep sites, which the government could then quickly protect by reforestation or by planting grass. But this conflicts with a rather dogmatic principle that calls for the Cuban state to buy up progressively all peasant land and never cede any to the peasants, even in temporary exchange. As a result, thousands of Sierra Maestra peasant families are still cultivating, and thus still eroding, many steep slopes. In addition, because they don't have enough land, particularly for growing their own food and feed for their pigs, they are often underemployed. With more level land at their disposal – and there is such land available – they could furnish meat to the neighbouring cities, where little is available. But peasant production is not approved of and is doomed to disappear.

In any event, the activities of the Che Guevara Brigade amounted to a genuine takeover of a rather faltering socialist agriculture by the army. A famous major is said to have remarked that 50,000 tractors, in more or less bad repair thanks to agricultural incompetence, made a marvelous training school. After March–April 1969 the men in charge of the *maquinaria* of the *granjas* were replaced by lieutenants, and the militarized tractor drivers were put on a fixed salary (thereby eliminating overtime pay) and a military schedule – twenty-five consecutive days of work, including Sundays, and five days of leave a month (when work permitted). Schools were established for tractor drivers and machine operators, and they also served to train young recruits. Plowing was done at top speed, and extraordinary records were cited – twenty-four and then seventy-two hours of continuous work! Tanks with their turrets removed were yoked together in twos with a heavy chain and used to uproot trees.

Agriculture thus became more than just an urgent problem to be solved; it became a magnificent training ground for the army. Militarization was urged not only to eliminate inefficiency and disorganization, but to cope with the passive resistance of a growing number of unwilling workers. The Cuban population was more and more under the control of the Party and the army, and it became increasingly difficult to distinguish between the two groups since they both wore uniforms and carried revolvers.

3. The death of the farm

The permanent personnel of, let us say, a *granja* of 2000 hectares of rice paddies, now consisted only of its manager, a storekeeper, the woman in charge of the canteen, and two old section supervisors, who were all but retired. Beginning in early 1969, all other work was done by brigades: more than a thousand men would move into an area to do a specific job, most of them for one or two weeks, sometimes for less than a week. The manager did what he could, but he was only there to execute the sometimes contradictory orders issued by shortwave radio (via permanent monitoring posts) or during impromptu inspections. Officials of the provincial plan, stationed eighty miles away, or even national officials, might arrive at any hour of the day or night. The section chiefs well understood their lack of importance and resigned themselves to it.

This 1969 campaign called for trial efforts in sugarcane and stock breeding: both failed. Units such as those I have described are no longer true agricultural enterprises with their own personnel, equipment, livestock, and, more important, capacity for initiative. Nobody was really responsible for the crops, to which were assigned successive waves of men arriving from various places, with equally nomadic equipment. A lot of time was lost in transporting and in setting up and organizing the work camps, which were all too often disbanded before they were running efficiently. It is possible to walk from an overcrowded camp where the equipment can't be used because there is too much of it, and to stumble across immense deserted fields where no one is around to even tell one where one is. This disorganized way of assigning equipment to mobile brigades that are separated from the agricultural production units resembles the infamous Soviet Mechanized Tractor Stations, which were always embroiled in disputes with "their" kolkhozes and finally had to be disbanded. Since the men are constantly on the move and live in barracks, they are unable to establish a family life and in addition are little drawn to agricultural work, which is badly paid and looked down on.

I have always argued that agriculture should be considered a local science. Though modern transformations have reduced the value of this dictum – for man is better able to master nature – they have not annuled it. Nature has to be well understood – in other words, studied closely. Decisions carried out in the field are now made in Cuba on a plan level, which is certainly closer than Havana was to its

granjas in 1963. But problems still come up at every step of the way –
rain, machine breakdowns, for instance – and these cannot be foreseen in even the best work-organization tables. To adapt to and
correct the situation local units need to be permitted more initiative,
and they especially need to have a minimum amount of production
means at their disposal. The principal justification for large-scale
plans is the full use of material, but Cuba's organizational structure
for agriculture has shown itself incapable of achieving that.

Another problem lies in the new emphasis on absolute monoculture. The major defects of the *granjas'* excessive diversification
have already been noted, but in passing too abruptly to the other
extreme – to absolute monoculture – Cuban planners overlooked
all the forms and advantages of crop rotation. Though there is certainly no absolute necessity to rotate crops, as the old agricultural
treatises urged, is it really necessary for the plans *always* to schedule
short-cycle plantings of bananas, pineapples, or papayas on the
same site? That remains to be seen. Banana trees are meant to last
a long time in Cuba, so they are widely separated, but most Cuban
crops are planted far apart. This made sense on poor and badly
watered soils, but planting and sowing will have to be much more
dense in order to derive the full benefit from new and expensive
production factors such as irrigation and the massive use of fertilizers.

The monoculture established by the plan arbitrarily separates
farming and stock farming, and overall provision is made only for
the use of cane leaves as fodder. Yet banana tree leaves are rich in
protein and could, with the frequent renewal of plantings, supply as
much fodder as a medium-yield pasture. (When temporary pastures
and crops are alternated, the land has to be divided up in long strips
to keep the cost of tractor plowing down, which calls for the use of
mobile electric fences.) The waste from market-garden crops is now
generally dumped, whereas it too could be used to feed cows and
pigs, as it is in the market garden near Athens: this would also increase stock density, the production of milk and meat, and natural
fertilizer resources. Pigs on the southern end of the Isle of Youth
now get all their food from Havana, but much of their fodder could
be produced on the spot, less expensively, and without the need and
cost of transport. The experience of centuries has proved that sugarcane is well adapted to a monoculture, that it can be planted on the
same soil indefinitely. But this does not mean that in some situations
there are not advantages in English ley farming – the rotation of

temporary pastures and annual crops, by which the soil can be recharged.

Of course the most up-to-date formulas used in the United States call for specialized farming, and Cubans are still very impressed by their northern neighbor, even though it is considered an enemy. But this separation of farming from stock farming did not appear in the United States until that country had reached a stage of overall economic development very much higher than that of Cuba in the early 1970s. Corn can be grown less expensively than grass in the corn belt south of Chicago, but the reverse is true in Cuba; transport is also considerably more expensive in Cuba, despite the island's small size.

4. The plans

In Bayamo, the provisional headquarters of Oriente province's *puesto de mando*, I was told how all the agriculture of the province was going to be organized. I saluted the apparent logic of the blueprint, but said I was "a little anxious" about how it would translate into practical and concrete terms in the field. "A *little* anxious!" repeated Captain Charandan, the official in charge of the plan, standing at attention (we were a mixed group of soldiers and civilians). "I'm *very* anxious."

Units of such scope, with an over-centralized direction of enterprises extending over tens or even hundreds of thousands of hectares, require men with extraordinary organizational abilities – of the sort who command high salaries in developed countries and who are not widely found until an advanced stage of development is reached. This kind of ability was still largely absent in Cuba in the late 1960s – as is normal, since this is a characteristic of underdevelopment. But what happened was that people who just couldn't do the job were asked to assume responsibilities that would be crushing even for experienced cadres. Officers were staffed by untrained advisors unwilling to listen to those who knew more than they did. Plans were quickly formulated on the basis of over-rapid or even non-existent studies.

Each unit receives and must apply a blueprint that has been worked out at the provincial (or national) headquarters. It is decided, for example, that fifty-four hectares of pangola pasture and twenty-seven hectares of harvested fodder have to feed 288 F1 milch cows. So specifications handed down from headquarters are used everywhere to build stables for this number of cows. Once the milking machines arrive, another type of building is prescribed. Pasture land is broken down into small plots, according to the model established by Voisin.* All areas are allotted the same intensity of agricultural production, although the naturally richer or better irrigated areas could move further ahead. Everybody keeps to the same developmental level, although the better educated, more astute unit chief should be free to move ahead and try new techniques. Finally, during a period of shortages something or other will always be missing and thus prevent the blueprints from working out according to plan. Southeast of Havana, in the Güines region, forty per cent of the *malangas* or *taros* so prized by Cuban housewives and their children were not harvested during the winter of 1968–9 because of the lack of men or machines. If the people from the cities had been mobilized by promising them fifteen or twenty per cent of the tubers they dug up, scarcely any of the crop would have been lost, for the additional volunteers needed would have been available. But here I am again incorrigibly recommending material incentives.

In short, the blueprints lack flexibility, they don't allow for enough initiative, and they don't pay sufficient attention to production costs. They also lack dynamism. (For example, it would be better to begin with modest stables that could be expanded as the pasture lands show their real potential.) But though the blueprints have to be flexible, the basic agricultural structure cannot with impunity continue to change so often. For nearly fifteen years Cuban agriculture has been subject to perpetual transformations, and the cost of each change has been high.

Let me cite another example of the very high cost of over-ambitious goals and the disorganization introduced by bureaucracy, even when it is militarized. Late in 1967 a French technical mission using French equipment – caterpillar scrapers, steam shovels, and road graders – was sent to Cuba to establish rice fields on horizontal terraces. By 1968 the Cubans had seen that the scrapers could be used for many other purposes. After a meeting with Castro on

* A Dieppe agriculturalist who had been able to establish this checkerboard pattern very economically because he had received heavy war indemnities. His book, *La Productivité de l'herbe*, contains some interesting facts, but Castro treated it as virtual scripture. Voisin died in Cuba and was given a national funeral. His name, like many of the heroes of the revolution, has been given to a number of Cuban institutions.

December 10, 1968 it was decided that before the May rains twenty-five scrapers would be used to create 1340 hectares of level rice fields south of Havana.

When on December 15 the French team received the preliminary plan, it learned that it would have to make do with ten scrapers and begin work on December 22. At the end of the year the anticipated site was shifted sixty kilometers because of (and we shall come back to this) a planned future highway. A month went by before a commission completed a very superficial topographical survey of the zone. On February 2 it was decided to limit the project to 330 hectares, but a more detailed topographical study was necessary before the equipment could be brought in. At a new meeting, the French expert was asked to limit himself to thirteen hectares – in other words, one per cent of the original project – and two scrapers. He nevertheless proposed to do fifty-four hectares, if he could get some topographers.

The students counted on for this job had in the interval been assigned elsewhere. However, thirty student rice specialists became available for the job on March 1. They had to wait two weeks for truck transportation to the site (they could have reached the site more quickly on foot). Once there they were taught practical topography in three days of intensive training – they abounded in good will and in two weeks they completed an impeccable relief map. These young people then received orders to return to their institute, and they left heartsick, persuaded that their work had been to no end. The Party representative swore on his honor as a revolutionary that he would make sure the work was finished. . . .

The scrapers arrived on the morning of April 19, but the students were no longer there to help the drivers carry out the leveling. (The drivers had to be taught their job from scratch, since the men who had been trained for it had been sent off to cut sugarcane.) One scraper broke down almost immediately; the other could not be used until the morning of April 21. By three in the afternoon an earlier-than-usual series of torrential rains began: it was too late for the job to be done. "We'll begin again in October."

At this point the French expert announced that he was "disgusted at just doing nothing and being paid for it with money accumulated by cutting down on food for the Cuban people," and refused to remain. (East European technicians are even more severe in their criticism of Cuban inefficiency and their own under-utilization, which scandalizes them at least as much.) In cooperative set-ups where everybody has an interest in seeing to it that things keep moving along, it hardly seems possible that the results could be worse. A better structure, adapted to the real situation (abilities, mental attitudes) and not to wishful thinking, would have permitted the purchase of less equipment and the accomplishment of more work. The resultant savings in time and foreign exchange would have made it possible to attack Cuba's food supply problem. In sum, Cuba's shortages are to a large extent due to the dogmatism of its leaders, although this doesn't mean that there aren't other contributing factors.

5. Castro and agriculture

In the final analysis Fidel Castro has confidence only in himself and is unable to delegate full responsibility. He remains the sole leader and feels that he has to see to and fix everything by himself. True, he is Cuba's moving spirit, his aims inspire effort, and his speeches still arouse a certain amount of enthusiasm – especially among his most faithful followers, the sugarcane workers. But when he starts promising the moon, many Cuban listeners turn off the radio because they no longer have faith. He wants to do everything by himself, and he has too many simultaneous ideas – every day and every moment – that he would like to put into action without examining the difficulties involved.

Let's follow him on one of his inspection tours. He finds a bridge in bad shape and gives orders for it to be repaired immediately. Fifty miles further along, his jeep bogs down (it's October) on a muddy road and there's trouble getting it unstuck. "See to it that a good asphalt road is built here." On another occasion (this time during the dry season) an entire agricultural zone is visibly suffering from the drought. "See to it that the area gets a little dam." At another place the crops appear neglected. "I want an agricultural school here."

I want, I want to do everything, immediately. All of which has its usefulness and attractiveness; Castro undeniably wants to do the right thing. His orders are noted down, the least of his words are respectfully absorbed (and often recorded on tape), everything is transmitted to the provincial headquarters, where the essential responsibilities are now assumed. (The progressive decentralization consists in not having to go to Havana quite so often.) But at the beginning of the year the unfortunate provincial technicians receive their official work programs, established by agreement between the planning junta and the technical ministries. To carry out these programs they have been assigned certain amounts of men and equipment, usually very closely estimated. The general disorganization reduces the potential of the means assigned, and in addition, programs are late in arriving. In addition Castro's personal ideas constitute another official program at least as imperative as the first. Attempts are therefore made to do everything, and what happens is that only a little of everything is done. This scattershot approach to work reduces productivity, and sometimes even completely eliminates it.

Once, talking to a Japanese rice grower, Castro learned that the secret behind Japan's ability to get three times as much rice per acre as Cuba does lies in the use of a strong fertilizer-spread very rich in potash, which prevents the rice from being beaten down by heavy rains or disease. A rational approach would have been to test this formula at the six small experimental stations that had just been set up in several provinces, and to use control plots to allow for soil differences. But, harshly critical of the Institute of Animal Husbandry for such opinions, Castro scornfully said, "Five experiments, five errors." His rejection of statistical calculation – without which the Philippine "miracle rice" so useful to Cuba could not have been developed – shows that some aspects of his scientific training leave much to be desired. This could be tolerated in a chief of state if he weren't so insistent on directing everything himself. In any case, during one of his inspection tours, he ordered a "test" of this Japanese formula – eighteen per cent nitrogen, twenty-four per cent phosphate, and eighteen per cent potash – on three large fields of more than a thousand hectares in all. The test was made in 1968-9, during the dry season, when since there is little risk of rain beating down the plants there is less need for potash. But the fact that it was Castro himself who ordered the test gave it many additional chances for success that had nothing to do with science. For "Fidel's test" the richest soil was of course chosen, the best seed, the optimal dates for sowing under optimal conditions, the most advanced and carefully carried-out cultivation techniques.

Castro is no longer content with his claims to military and political fame and his undeniable value as a human being. He has to feel himself recognized as the leader in both scientific research and agricultural practice. He's the man who knows everything. Now that the peasants, who were once open-mouthed in their admiration, have been brushed aside with a wave of the hand, he wants to show researchers (for example, Preston and Willis in animal husbandry) and plan officials that he is the man most capable – if not the only one capable – of making a synthesis between science and common sense.

Again with rice: an expert suggested putting seed beds under plastic tents to multiply new rice strains more quickly. Castro mobilized two hundred Party volunteers for a month to seed six hectares of terraced rice fields (when there is so much level land in Cuba). To hasten the growth of this rice he interpreted the technician's advice in his own way and installed – "to keep the rice constantly warm" – three thousand big spotlights, each set on an approximately twelve-foot post. He forgot that hot air rises and that too much exposure to light retards the ripening of certain rice strains. The most serious aspect of the situation was that no member of his technical team dared point out his many mistakes.

As difficulties increase Castro asks his fellow Cubans not to linger in the present but to turn their eyes toward a horizon that moves further and further away – it is now, for example, 1980. (By definition the horizon is a line that moves into the distance as we approach.) He traces a more and more idyllic picture of that future – a future within their grasp if they accept a program that becomes increasingly far-fetched – especially to anyone whose first thoughts are for the Cubans' daily rice needs.

Nevertheless he does have an understanding of agriculture, and many of his decisions are justified. After having decided on the priority of agriculture, he was and remains an important agent of the acceleration of agronomic progress. But he exaggerated the priority on sugar and, above all, alienated many valuable technicians, whom he disillusioned and eventually drove into opposition. The man who opposes Castro's ideas is quickly rejected, and as a result when Castro sets forth a mistaken proposition nobody dares oppose him if he wants to hold on to his job, as is usually the case. His entourage seems to be cowed by a mixture of fear and admiration.

The first plan had in part placed the initial rice fields to the south of Havana in the Matanzas clays, soils too gritty, too permeable for rice, but very fertile for other crops. After much trouble the French technicians succeeded in having the rice plantings shifted to a marshy zone. But it is across these rice fields that Castro now wants to build a southern highway. Tens of thousands of tons of concrete will have to be sunk into the mud as deeply as they will go, or tens of thousands of truckloads of earth will have to be brought in to build a dike-road that can still never be strong enough. Somewhat farther north, the Matanzas clays rest on a bed of limestone. If the highway were built here it would cost much less, would be better, and would pass closer to centers of habitation! "I want it to be possible to see rice on both sides of the road," Castro is said to have insisted. If this is true, it is a remark unworthy of a leader concerned with the economy and therefore well-being of his people. It is not the reply of a socialist, but of a *grand seigneur*.

The port of Havana must increase its handling facilities because increased crops (citrus fruits, pineapples, bananas, coffee,vegetables, etc.) and the new factories will considerably enlarge its traffic. The Institute of Physical Planning found an excellent site for a new zone of warehouses immediately fronting the harbor – a site requiring no major demolition, well served by auto and railroad facilities, etc., etc. But with a stroke of his pen, Castro decided that this sector would be treated like the rest of the area around Havana: planted with fruit trees and interspersed with coffee shrubs. The "temporary" aspect of this plan did not last very long and most of the coffee shrubs, moribund, have already been uprooted. Each of the remaining fruit trees – and many are gone – has been surrounded with a protective grill, and Castro now wants grass and sheep in the area. (Why sheep at the gates of a city so much in need of fresh milk?) This project too must have been planned with foreign visitors in mind, since many of them are easily impressed. Visitors would first be shown Havana, the former capital of prostitution and gambling – the center of all capitalist vices – then, after a few miles, they would arrive at the foot of reforested hills with artificial lakes and anti-erosion terraces (sadly lacking a little farther on), and, in the foreground, sheep grazing in orchards! Could there be a more idyllic, more Marie-Antoinette-like spectacle! The contrast is likely to please the progressive city dweller, especially if he is predisposed to admire and expecting to be shown an idyllic image of socialist accomplishments.

In July 1969 the Havana–Santiago de Cuba highway was begun. The first lap from the capital has eight lanes, four in each direction. When the project was discussed at the Institute of Physical Planning, a major – only somebody of that rank would have taken such license – timidly observed that the revolution wasn't concerned with private automobiles (there still are some) and that therefore two lanes in each direction would amply suffice for all foreseeable

future traffic (trucks, buses, service vehicles, tractors, etc.). All that
need be done was to make provision for eventual expansion. But
Castro had just read two handsome books on the Olympic Games in
Japan, and they had contained superb photos of highways and inter-
changes. "The Japanese did it. Why shouldn't we?" Everybody
exchanged amazed looks at this extraordinary response, more suited
to a *caballero* than to an economist aware of the present dis-
proportion between the Cuban economy and the enormous power of
Japan.

As a starting point for the two highways going from Havana to
the east and to the west, Castro proposed the Plaza de la
Revolucion, and with one stroke of a red pencil indicated this on a
plan over which experts had labored for weeks. His route required
a wide avenue – city traffic would have augmented the flow on the
two highways – giving access to the port. To do this a good part of
one of Havana's old quarters would have had to be leveled. Castro
conceded this point, and agreed that the highway should begin at the
port. His next mark would have made it necessary for a hospital to
be razed. He agreed to bypass the hospital, but his third indication
for how he wanted the highway to be is the one that has been carried
out.

If Castro had Che Guevara's mentality – which is far from the case
– one might ask: "If he were voluntarily to give up leadership of the
country, would its development profit?" The question cannot be
lightly decided, because this *caballero* is also the *caballo*, the horse,
that for better or worse drags the Cubans forward; it is he who puts
the women to work, who urges the country on, who meddles in
everything. What seems called for is a Central Committee, aware of
its responsibilities, able to make him understand that on the basis
of a partial view of the overall situation he cannot decide on every
detail without upsetting an order of priorities established after long
consideration. It is indispensable that he should respect the responsibilities that he himself has delegated, and above all that he
should make use of available ability instead of insisting first on
political qualifications, on revolutionary awareness. On October 20,
1969 he said, "May intelligence and ability, united to patriotism
and conscience, prevail." Let him heed this counsel.

The situation is certainly not that of a classical South American
dictatorship, and those in the United States who often compare
the present regime to that of Batista are wrong. Batista wanted
power so that he and his clique could profit from it. He depended on

the United States and made every possible concession to it. Castro defends Cuba's national interests; he has restored the dignity of the country's poorest people – the agricultural workers – and of its most despised – the blacks and the mulattoes. Such things cannot be measured in economic terms. He does all he can for the people, for their education and their health. But in doing all this he follows his own ideas, convinced that they are the best. Thus he assumes un-checked personal power, and this fosters a courtier-like approach in those around him. When he throws his beret on the ground and flies into one of his rages everybody quakes and fears reprisals.

Castro is an extraordinary man – he would be an altogether extraordinary one if he could master himself better, listen, reflect more, and stop promising the moon – and he can feel and articulate the aspirations and potentialities of the Cuban people. He is an intuitive man who understands things quickly but who is very susceptible to influences. His entourage is made up of doctrinaires, not all of whom are Cuban, and they have postulated debatable philosophical-political principles that have to be accepted as revealed truth. Instead of beginning scientifically with the *observa-tion* of fact from which rules of action can be deduced, they try to bend facts, to transform man and nature. Until democratic methods of rule are developed in Cuba the psychology of officials will be an important study for the future of the Cubans. Before cautiously approaching such thorny questions, we must first consider some of the unusual characteristics of Cuban socialism that make it of special interest.

The first of these is the *new man*. We must try to understand his nature and ask ourselves if he can contribute to Cuba's rapid development more efficiently than he does now. Cuba has made massive investments, but they have not yet led to a significant increase in production. Man is still the decisive element – as the Chinese have reminded us. But the majority of Cubans are no longer as sure of this as they were in 1959 and 1960. They are "disenchanted" and they have good reason to be so.

How can the voice of the people be heard in high places? Murmurs from below can be heard at many meetings, and some echoes have reached Castro. But they are muffled by his entourage, which, without always being aware of it, bears a great responsibility. Svetlana Alliluyeva judiciously reminds us that Stalin wasn't the only one responsible for the abuses of Stalinism. The proof is that they have survived him.

7

Rapprochement with the USSR

1. The rear guard, crime, and the party

Che Guevara called the construction of socialism a *"strange* and thrilling drama,"* seeing in it something of a departure from the normal, something perhaps irrational, the origin of which stemmed from the guerilla struggle. "The attitude of our combatants already showed the man of the future." But since combat exaltation never lasts, Che Guevara looked for "the formula by which this heroic attitude could be perpetuated in daily life". Realizing finally that it could not become established fast enough, he preferred to return to the heroic life: he wanted to avoid "the temptation to turn to material interest as a lever in economic development."

In this search for a new man – magnificent and exhilarating indeed if it were really to succeed – "the road is long and full of obstacles. . . . In the avant-garde there is a qualitative change that makes them self-sacrificing, the others are less conscious and must be subjected to pressures of a certain intensity." However, if this "dictatorship of the proletariat over the victorious class" is to be justified, one must be certain that the avant-garde is moving in the right direction; one must be able to define a political truth, an ideal society. For myself, I believe that such a task is absolutely impossible.

Che Guevara specified that for socialist man to become complete it was necessary to "accentuate his conscious *participation*, individually and collectively, in all the mechanisms of leadership and production." If, as I was told, the military society that I saw on the Isle of Youth and in the Camagüey Columna prefigures communism, this sort of communism is devilishly close to army life. In that case we are no longer dealing with a future society, for the army is a very old institution that goes back for millennia. This military society, several aspects of which have been described in this book, follows a path leading away from participation; it leads to a hierarchized society with an authoritarian leadership, headed by a personal power that decides all problems, political, economic, and technical.

Che Guevara asked that "the masses be mobilized by means of a fundamentally ethical instrument that would nevertheless make correct use of material incentives, especially those of a social order." C. R. Rodriguez emphasized that it must not therefore be thought that money would disappear (as one minister thought, who saw in this disappearance a solution to his credit difficulties!). After Castro's speech of July 26, 1968 he observed that there was "some haste to adopt measures that would contribute to making money less important, but there was no question of eliminating it." Rodriguez knew that there were still two groups in Cuba: the highly aware avant-garde and the rest, the majority. (He knew that this clearly distinguishes Cuba from Korea, where he was "profoundly impressed" by the capacity for work and by the responsibilities undertaken by the mass of the people.) The direction taken in Cuba offers unquestionable advantages for a society of this type, especially for agricultural production units: it makes it unnecessary to check on the quantity and quality of each man's work before deciding on his remuneration. In the USSR, endless calculations like these swelled kolkhoz bureaucracy and monopolized an excessive part of production – a sort of socialist surplus value. In China the workers' collectives decide on remuneration, and this reduces the bureaucracy.

But in order to be efficacious Cuba's orientation requires that the mass make real progress and that it participate more and more in planning and leadership. We have seen that Cuba is turning its back on this second point, and, as to the first point, the situation is not very encouraging either.

In mid-1969 Jorge Risquet, Minister of Labor, emphasized in a speech at the National Congress on Labor Justice that "undisciplined work, absenteeism, and negligence in working are *increasing* phenomena against which a struggle must be undertaken on many fronts." As he saw it, "the negligence of a worker is also that of a supervisor, who is unable to demand from his subordinates that their duties be undertaken with the necessary energy." This was an appeal to the reinforcement of military discipline, rather than to the revolutionary conscience of the worker. A month later, in September, according to *Le Monde*, "the Cuban government promulgated a law under which each worker would have a dossier and work book in which would be noted the places in which he has worked – his comings and goings and transfers." Risquet specified that "in a society based on merit, there is no more lasting moral incentive or stronger *moral sanction* than to have entered in the dossier the *behavior* and *attitude* of each worker, his contribution to the common task." Where Che Guevara spoke only of moral *incentive*, Risquet added moral *sanction*; given the atmosphere, it might well be more than moral. And it appeared to be not just a rearguard but the majority of the masses that had adopted a "backward" stance.

In March of the same year Castro had rightly emphasized that "men will find their greatest incentives in the content of their work ... but [that] this motivation is linked to their cultural level.... Interest and passion are aroused as soon as technique comes into play." But he had no patience with crime, which was rising sharply. "It is even possible that we may one day be faced with the necessity of radically eliminating incurable, incorrigible, and inveterate delinquents." A headline in *Granma* not long afterward proclaimed "The Death Struggle Against Crime," and a *death* struggle was what it was. The National Congress on Internal Order noted a strong increase in thefts – evidently even greater than official figures had indicated – and attributed it to the shortages that made it possible to profit from the sale of stolen goods. But it was also, more simply, attributable to an attempt to obtain necessities. Law 1908 calls for the application of *capital punishment* for armed robbery of occupied premises by inveterate criminals. "The conception of a minor will have to be revised," Castro noted. "If at sixteen a young man can undertake military service, die for his country, why, if he commits a crime, should he not bear penal responsibility?" Here too we may ask ourselves what Che Guevara would have thought of this. Castro's position on this point hardened; instead of appealing to conscience, he now threatened even the very young.

Castro is of course right to worry about "the academic backwardness of the still large number of children who do not go to school, the non-adaptability of these future illiterates among a people that will have more and more skills." But to go on, as he does, to present delinquency as a vestige of the past, a relic of capitalism, seems to me a basic error that can have fearful consequences. In the Soviet Union delinquency hardly seems on the decline although most of the population have few or no memories of the capitalistic period. Though it is suggested that children of sixteen be severely punished,* no mention is made of the fact that those who were that age in 1972 were only two in 1958, the last year of capitalism.

In substance, Castro is saying that it is now possible for everyone to earn a living, that there is no more poverty. This is on the whole true, if we are talking about extreme poverty. But there are poor people in Cuba, people who are considerably more disadvantaged than the others, especially during this period of general shortages. Castro who lives well, is not aware of this; the same was true of Che Guevara, who at the end of his stay in Cuba and after he had been reproached for being unaware of the food shortages, had decided "to eat like the people."

The passive resistance of an increasing faction of the farming, rural, and urban masses seems to stem largely from a disappointment with this state of affairs which almost equals the wild enthusiasm of 1959–60 that had engendered such unprecedented hopes. For a long time they struggled against disillusion because they wanted to return neither to Batista nor to Yankee hegemony. For a long time they tried to believe with all their hearts. But the constant repetition of wasted effort, failure, foolishness, and mistakes gave rise to the fear that their ever-increasing sacrifices would lead to nothing but accentuated poverty. As this threat took shape and bore down on them, some heartsick workers were forced into a politics of despair despite themselves. "The worse things go, the faster we'll be finished with these incompetents," they may say. This disgust is felt even by the young technicians, many of whom still think the disorder stems from the fact that Castro hasn't the time to see and attend to everything. "If Fidel had known about that, there would have been hell to pay. . . . " But the adults who thought this way in 1967 no longer do.

Here are some examples:

At the Sancti Spiritus rice plan I saw twenty-six tractors in the fields, only one of which was being used. The drivers were supposed to plow the submerged soil and also use the front-mounted blades to repair the small retention dikes surrounding each plot of land. Only the one tractor still had the blade, so it alone was in operation. The others could have been used to plow, of course, and

---

* A young sentinel guarding some new rice plantings had one night let cows graze amidst them, and Castro wanted to have him shot. He was restrained with difficulty by being reminded that the grazing would in fact encourage the plant growth. Once over his rage, he agreed to have the sentence changed to fifteen years on a prison farm.

the single tractor with the blade could have fixed the dikes, but the tractor drivers weren't very concerned. "We're not on piece work," they said, and went swimming in the canal.

Or again, when twenty-four Soviet tractors arrived in Oriente province in spring 1969, equipped with headlights for night work, some of the tractor drivers on night duty unscrewed the headlights and dropped them into the canals. This isn't a case of CIA interference, or of pro-American or counter-revolutionary sabotage, but of simple self-defense by exhausted people, a case of resistance to authority when it demands efforts that some – those not heroically inclined – feel are excessive and above all badly paid.

Rodriguez has said that if such incidents are to be eliminated it must be remembered that man is the decisive element, the most precious capital. To get real agricultural workers, it will be necessary to build them decent living quarters and to take greater care of their comfort. The workers should not have to complain to foreign visitors.

2. Democratic discussion in the Party

Cuban communism already has one feature that is not very unusual. In all communist parties – except in Yugoslavia, in Czechoslovakia 1968, and during the Chinese cultural revolution (three very different things) – the freedom of discussion and popular control advised by Lenin have been forgotten.* All that has been retained is so-called "democratic" centralism, interpreted so that it is most favorable to the establishment of an unlimited dictatorship of personal power, in which directives are transmitted from top to bottom and no significant allowance is made for popular demands to be transmitted from the bottom to the top. The directive group isn't "involved" with the masses, doesn't make them participate, and is insufficiently concerned with their needs.

Che Guevara once cited Castro's dialogue with the people as a good way to retain contact with the masses. I heard the speeches Castro gave on May 20, 1960 and on July 14, 1969: only the first attempted the rudiments of a dialogue, and even this was skilfully manipulated by Castro. The second was no longer anything but a monologue, with only one interruption from the audience, an inter-

---

* "Hadn't you been promised fifty years ago . . . that the truth would be stated immediately, that the masses would openly debate everything?" Alexander Solzhenitsyn, "Open Letter of November 1969."

ruption that was quickly waved aside as inopportune. When I told a high Party official that I was going to write a constructive critical essay on the Cuban economy, he remarked, in the presence of witnesses, that a mechanism for democratic discussion was not even provided within the Party.

He no doubt intended that I should repeat his comment, and that's what I've done. But what else did he intend? He was probably not very happy about the large number of secret police in the Party. I also had the impression that there was still clique fighting among Party officials – especially between the majors who had come with Castro from the Sierra and the militants formed by the traditional Communist Party, who are often closer to the Soviet Union. (It was Rodriguez who was delegated as an observer at the June 1969 Moscow conference of communist parties.)* These last are particularly concerned about the militarization of the Cuban economy and society – and above all about the increased power of the military – since a real hunt seems to have been organized recently against many of the old communists, who have been purged from their command posts.

In May 1969 Armando Hart, an official in charge of Party organization, discussed "the gravity of the under-utilization of the labor force" at the closing session of a provincial organizational meeting in Havana province. But, to eliminate the problems caused by this, Hart proposed an increase in the number of Party members; yet it was never, until recently, suggested that members be chosen on the basis of technical or professional competence. Personality, social relations, or moral qualities were not to be considerations for refusing an applicant, said Hart. "We cannot organize a party of archangels," as Che Guevara used to say. The most important thing was the man's past history as a combatant, "that he have a clear political understanding, that he fully, totally, and completely accept the line of the Cuban revolution." In other words, it was total submission to a political line defined without the participation of the members that had become the essential quality. Nowhere in the speeches of Hart or Castro did I find an allusion to democratic discussion within the Party, as Che Guevara had urged.

Submission logically leads to a strongly hierarchized obedient,

* "Considering the development of Cuban mentality, Rodriguez is our Bukharin," I was told by one of Castro's former ministers who has now been relegated to a minor position. "He's more like our Mikoyan," replied somebody else – in which case his career is apt to be longer.

military society.* For capitalist alienation this kind of society sub-
stitutes another form of the loss of essential liberties, and this loss
increases the weight of material difficulties that could in part be
avoided. It is for this reason that one must emphasize that
Cuban society offers only some elements of socialism and the
reduction of certain social injustices. Submission does not make for
the aware individual, and collective participation called for by
Che Guevara, and which is the essential basis of socialism – as
important as the collective appropriation of the means of production.

In point of fact many Party members more or less just buzz from
here to there and then boast "Objective accomplished," although in
fact it has been accomplished by others. It should be remembered
that Lenin counseled democratic centralism as the kind of organization necessary *for the takeover of power*. It is certainly the wrong one
for the promotion of economic development once victory is achieved,
however. It is too easily transformed into a hierarchized structure
utilized as a means of social climbing, not only by revolutionaries
but also (sometimes especially) by ambitious people more or less
devoted to the people. This is happening in Cuba. It can only be
avoided by popular control and the total absence of privileges for
Party cadres; material incentives will have to be eliminated for
the political avant-garde before they are taken from the base. Yes,
but then would the cadres consent to the watch-dog role so often
forced on them?

3. Stalinism with a human face: the army "appraises" poets

In the gray spring of 1969, a spring considerably less sunny than
that of 1968, young Czechs defined Husak's "normalization"
efforts as Stalinism with a human face; it could be compared to
Kadar's attempts at "normalization" after the 1956 Hungarian
revolt. As I pointed out to some oppositionists – adherents of the
Cuban Revolution who had become disillusioned with its recent
military orientation and the accentuation of personal dictatorship†

---

* Party officials in Cuba get an information bulletin that keeps them up to
date on the international situation and on domestic problems. The people get
no such information, not even ordinary Party members. It's like the Middle
Ages – nothing must disturb the faith of the humble.

† The milder oppositionists still respect Castro, but they think he is surrounded by incompetents. (Many in the USSR said the same of Stalin after
1930.)

– Cuba does not have a Stalinist regime, inasmuch as our meetings were not disturbed by the police (who had no trouble keeping tabs on me through my chauffeur). Yet the police do not lack help, for "vigilance" is a quality most highly urged by official posters.

"Awareness doesn't come with wealth," proclaim many of these posters, and it's true. But does it come with vigilance, with the increasing control of neighborhoods by Revolutionary Defense Committees (CDRs), standing in for and helping the official police? Everybody belongs to the CDRs,* unless he wants to miss out on many advantages. (Two unarmed women assigned to night patrol by the CDR ask what they should do in the face of a determined thief: they are told to shout.) But the political official, the informer who does the denouncing, is a hated person. "If he got paid well, like the leaders, you could understand him. But he eats as badly as the rest of us, so he ought to keep his trap shut." Capitalist society denied the worker his dignity, and it was precisely this dignity that was one of the most valuable conquests of the Cuban revolution; police inquisition again denies it to the poorest worker.

A mulatto housewife in a working-class neighborhood, seeing that I was an interested foreigner, had kindly invited me in; later I wanted to thank her. After telling my chauffeur not to follow me in the car, I walked past the CDR post, where an old Cubano-African woman on duty asked me where I was going. "I'm just walking around looking at these wonderful gardens." When I passed the post on my way back, a police car was there, and my driver, looking somewhat embarrassed, was being asked for explanations. A guest of Castro who visits working-class neighborhoods without official guides is after all suspicious.

Of course precautions have to be taken against sabotage, but the primary emphasis is now on the supervision of the population and on training it by means of pointless guard duty. Given this atmosphere it is easier to understand why poet Heberto Padilla's book, *Fuera de juego*, though it had been awarded the Casa de las Americas poetry prize by a Cuban jury, could not be published without a special preface by the Union of Cuban Writers and Artists. Toeing the official line the Union expressed its "disagreement with the contents, which it judges to be ideologically contrary to our revolution," although the most famous of the Casa de las Americas

---

* Which do have some positive functions in matters of education and health. And there are still enemies of the revolution.

jurists, Haydee Santamaria, who fought in the Sierra and is now director of the Casa, publicly affirmed the right of literary judges to the free expression of literary judgement. At a certain level, it is still possible to express an opinion.

"A poet is not someone with whom one talks here," said Padilla. "There is no political organization within which one can discuss the real problems of writers. According to its statues, UNEAC is supposed to change presidents every two years. As it happens, the same president has been in office for seven years, and the staff has been changed without consulting the mass of writers. My book was strongly attacked, often with accusations of a police nature, especially in the army publication *Verde Olivo*, but I have no opportunity to reply to these attacks." These attacks against the intellectual rebels have also been taken up by *Granma*; thus the army point of view on this important issue – the relationship between a revolution and its intellectuals – has become the official one.*

The UNEAC staff goes to work in the fields every Wednesday. They travel in a handsome bus, and once there they eat well: fish, chopped meat, real milk, coffee. There are twenty-six in the group, and while four women tend to the cooking, the others put in eight hours weeding four rows of cane about 450 feet long, less than a fourth of what a regular worker does. However, those UNEAC members who put in some twenty consecutive days in the field do manage about half the norm. So that the ten-million-ton *zafra* could be celebrated, all UNEAC members were assigned for nine months to a sugar refinery – not to work with their hands, but to watch what was going on, so they could write about it if the spirit moved them.

4. New man or model soldier?

What then is happening to those special and original characteristics of Cuban socialism that I had noted with such pleasure in 1960 and 1963, and that I had so eagerly returned to restudy in 1969, even though I didn't agree with all of them? They are being reduced to a

---

* In the spring of 1971 Heberto Padilla was kept under arrest for thirty-seven days, at the end of which he "admitted" having been in gross error in adopting counter-revolutionary positions and providing information to CIA agents such as myself and K. S. Karol (whose political analyses in his book, *Guerrillas in Power* complement my economic analyses).

militaristic society, one in which Raul Castro often repeats the army's byword: "At your orders, commander-in-chief – for no matter what, no matter where, and under all circumstances."

As we have seen, a short-tempered Castro can abuse this attitude. And the militarism of Cuba today hardly conforms to the spirit of what in 1959–60 was called a *rebel* army in order to underline the basic difference between it and the traditional South American army. Of course there are still many happy differences, but not as far as discipline is concerned. The overall picture finally begins to resemble certain aspects of Stalinism – without the terror, but with a widespread use of police. Another feature of Stalinism which is present is the simplification of theory. Before one has been in Cuba very long one finds a darkening of that potentially magnificent but ever-receding vision of the new man living in a fraternal society. Many communist officials convey a pretty poor idea of it.

"Two thousand years of Christian preaching aimed at improving man have had only limited results," I said to Monsignor Zachi, who represents the Vatican in Cuba and is on the best of terms with Fidel Castro – a mark in the latter's favor as well. "Oh, very limited," replied the Monsignor. As I have read somewhere, we have passed from the cave age straight to the barracks age. This latter development is having an impudent triumph in Cuba, where posters celebrate the pride of the country – the little *camillitos* (disciples of Camillo Cienfuegos), cadets in the officer-training school who from childhood on have been prepared as future leaders – and not only of soldiers.

The responses to such a situation have been a Party Central Committee designated from above, a Party congress that is never convened, and a constitution that has not been drafted, in spite of many promises. Only the leaders have the right to point out slackers or troublesome situations; at the base, nobody can criticize the leaders (as is possible in China under certain conditions) without immediately being accused of lacking revolutionary spirit. This situation impoverishes the standardized and conformist Cuban press, which every day consecrates at least a page to the exploits of the heroic epoch – from Moncada to guerilla warfare in the Sierra and the Bay of Pigs.

In 1969 the newspaper *El Mundo* was fused with *Granma*, official organ of the Central Committee of the Cuban Communist Party, the only organism able to speak up in Cuba. Reporters on its evening edition, *Juventud Rebelde*, bitterly complain of the censorship that prevents them from making it into a more interesting paper. Censorship is the original sin of communist societies, which think they can protect themselves by staving off criticism. In the end they are self-defeating, and that can only be regretted.

The organ for theoretical discussion, the monthly *Cuba Socialista*, was shut down in February 1967 "until such a time as the Central Committee has defined the Party's theoretical line." Everybody is still waiting. It had formerly been devoted to stimulating discussions of theory, for example, between Che Guevara and Bettelheim. In a neo-Stalinistic set-up issues of this sort are carefully avoided, for they may quickly lead to questioning the supreme wisdom of the commander-in-chief.

Little by little a special aspect of this *new man* begins to emerge, an aspect already glimpsed on the posters at the entrance to the Isle of Youth. The new man is a model soldier, ever-obedient to his leaders, determined on self-sacrifice, and joyfully accepting all difficulties and assignments. Children are enrolled in organizations as soon as they are ten. Adolescents and adults from fifteen to fifty-five have to mount guard before just about every heap of bricks – a bitter joke and one whose sole function is conditioning. Isolated for two years in the gloomy Minas del Frio teachers' training school, young teachers are subjected to programs that smack of the convent or the barracks – another isolation for conditioning purposes. Machete work for everybody is also a way in which resistance is broken down. The same goes for rationing, less difficult to tolerate for those who accept the system: "Work and shut up." The leaders are always right: "Fidel doesn't argue." "Change man," said Che Guevara. "Dominate nature," adds the poster. But aren't they now trying to *dominate man*? Though adults may resist, the young most often accept. Wasn't Che Guevara's decision to leave influenced by the fact that he had begun to understand where this orientation was leading? You can't just put together a "new man" who has all the qualities required by an abstract society. Man is a biological being who has aptitudes that can be developed, used, and increased by leaders of men; it is necessary to use existing aptitudes and limit the manifestation of anti-social tendencies – that's the job of education. Education is always preferable to constraint. If Castro would rid himself of his mystics and utopians and surround himself with real representatives of the people and better technicians, he could lead the Cuban people to prosperity, expanding the faculties of an active and intelligent population.

Like a Christian proclaiming his faith, especially when he's not all that sure of it, Castro loudly insists, "I have complete faith in Marxism." Nevertheless, he has not authorized the publication of Che Guevara's complete works because some of them severely criticize men still in power, as well as methods still being employed. Nor is all of Marx authorized. Actually, Marx is an author dangerous to all regimes, for he wrote: "*The censored press* daily praises the results of government policy, but because one day necessarily contradicts another, the press *constantly lies*; it must even deny that it is aware of lying and must renounce all shame." I challenge *Granma* to publish that sentence.

5. Re-Stalinization and rapprochement with the Soviet Union

When Castro visits the University of Havana the atmosphere appears to be cordial. (He cannot be reproached for the way in which he surrounds himself with bodyguards, for there are powerful interests that would be all too happy to have him disappear.) But in fact the general atmosphere is such that a student or an oppositionist professor could be dismissed for stating his opinions before members of the Young Communist League or university federation.

This is, in fact, what happened during the big 1964-5 purges. A student who merely refused to participate in a vote was beaten up as he was walking down the university steps. "It's disgraceful," they said, "that some people should sully the steps of an institution for which Che shed his blood." Poor Che – now that he's dead, he can be made to say anything. A woman professor who had merely mentioned the existence of certain kinds of rationing in Russia was expelled shortly after Castro's July 26, 1968 speech, the charge against her being that she had "too much influence on her students." A person in the school of medicine was also expelled: he worked hard over his books but didn't work in the fields often enough. Outspoken nonconformists were finally unable to continue their studies; one after another they left the country, depriving Cuba of those dissenting elements that are indispensable to progress.

This neo-Stalinist militarization was accompanied by a more and more marked rapprochement with the Soviet Union. We have come a long way from the day – January 2, 1968 – when Castro publicly attributed the gas rationing to Russia's refusal to increase deliveries (of course Cuba had not furnished the promised sugar).

A few days later Castro proclaimed:

There can be nothing more anti-Marxist than dogma, the petrifaction of ideas. Some who speak in the name of Marxism are like fossils. Marxism must develop, and not become ossified; it must behave like a revolutionary force and not like a pseudo-revolutionary church. When elements of the clergy become revolutionaries, are we to resign ourselves to seeing sectors of Marxism turn into an ecclesiastical force? We hope that saying so won't lead to our excommunication or to the Holy Inquisition.

This political line, so markedly different from that of the Soviet Union, introduced the trial of Anibal Escalante (already convicted once in 1962) and his thirty-five comrades in February 1968. During the trial Raul Castro emphasized that Escalante maintained communication with Moscow and had written to the editor of *Izvestia*, painting a catastrophic picture of Cuba's economic and social conditions and claiming that "the anti-communist petty bourgeoisie has taken over the revolution." But the trial was scarcely over (and Escalante condemned to fifteen years in prison) when Castro, his point made, realized, or was made to realize, that Cuba couldn't do without the more than five million annual tons of Soviet oil, 100,000 tons a week – infusions of blood and gold: a tanker every fifty hours!

The rapprochement was clearly affirmed in a speech of August 23, 1968 – though many in Havana had expected it to contain a severe attack against the Soviet Union. In it Castro approved of the recent invasion of Czechoslovakia. Though he expressed serious reservations about the Novotny government – an indirect criticism of Soviet re-Stalinization – for Russia the essential thing about the speech was Castro's approbation, even if this didn't amount to unconditional alignment.

So it is easy to see why the Cubano-Soviet Friendship Association was not founded until April 22, 1969 – ten years after the triumph of the revolution, nine years after Mikoyan's visit of friendship, and eight years after the proclamation of Cuba as a socialist society. And the visit of a unit of the Soviet fleet to Cuba in July, and the arrival of Marshal Grechko in November accentuated the political, and above all military rapprochement. It was relatively easy to reach an understanding on the military terrain; comrades-in-arms were saluted, no mention was made of the withdrawal of missiles after October 1962. Led by their vice-admiral, the Soviet sailors went to the Matanzas area, where they symbolically cut sugarcane alongside their Cuban comrades, led by Castro.

At the time this Cuban-Soviet friendship clearly signified an implicit condemnation of Chinese policy, whose principal enemy was the USSR. However, this position was not officially confirmed, and Cuba continued to deplore the Sino-Soviet division in the face of the common enemy, American imperialism.

The two countries that Cuba most wants to identify with are North Vietnam and North Korea. Cuban leaders often told me how much the heroic resistance of the Vietnamese had aroused their people's enthusiasm for work, thereby making a positive and decisive contribution to their development. There have also been numerous gestures of friendship toward North Korea. But the Cuban-Soviet understanding may only sharpen Cuba's differences with China, which have never really been straightened out. Cuba's position here is markedly different from North Vietnam's. The latter has attempted at least until 1970 to establish a difficult but scrupulous balance between China and Russia.

On January 2, 1969 Castro's comments on the Soviet Union had apparently completely changed their tone of the previous year:

> We must point out, at a time when we foresee success and a magnificent future for our country, what the solidarity of the socialist camp and especially that of the Soviet Union has meant to us. We have sometimes had disagreements about different criteria, and we have expressed them in all honesty. But with the same honesty we have to emphasize [a year ago he hadn't "had" to do anything] that [Soviet] food shipments were decisive for this country during the first years, when our production was declining. The same is true for the shipments of arms, when we were facing the greatest threats. These armaments are very expensive, they are worth more than all the equipment used in our development, and we received them *free*. . . . When we have lacked competent personnel, we have received the necessary technicians. . . . When we had mediocre harvests and were not able to make the deliveries corresponding to our imports, the imports were not affected. . . . We must in all justice say that this aid was *decisive*.*

* In Mexico it is said that Cuban socialism "is still on the bottle" – the Soviet **bottle**, that is.

In March, 1969 Raul Castro emphasized that an "order from the leader is the law incarnating the will and the command of the country." He asked that "soldiers be trained to friendship with the sister armies of socialist countries; especially the Great Soviet Army, whose representatives daily work at the side of our officers and also harvest the fruits of our common efforts." Reading these lines one might think that there was no longer the slightest disagreement between the two countries, but this was not true.

Though Cuba had refused to take part in the preparations for the Congress of Communist and Workers' Parties – finally held, after numerous difficulties, in Moscow in June 1969 – the Central Committee of the Cuban Party sent an observer delegation headed by C. R. Rodriguez. In a speech at the Congress Rodriguez said that he had come so that his "absence would not become a weapon in the hands of the enemies of the worldwide revolutionary unity of communists," but he emphasized "the deformations that weaken Marxist-Leninist conceptions and the opportunist positions that we consider the principal present danger." To attack "opportunism" in June 1969 was to approve the occupation of Czechoslovakia, Soviet re-Stalinization, the condemnation of liberal writers, etc. Yet at the same time he underlined "the internal divisions of the socialist system," which Moscow preferred to pass over in silence, and denounced "the establishment and enlargement of diplomatic relations between socialist countries and Latin American governments . . . maneuvers aimed at dividing the masses." He also declared that there is "too little discussion of the more and more frequent outbreaks of rebellion among young workers and students – a fact linked to the reluctance of some sectors of the communist movement to admit that the material situation of the working class in developed countries has been ameliorated largely at the expense of the people of Africa, Asia, and Latin America." Rodriguez asked that "the importance of the rebellion of youth . . . in the liquidation of capitalism be better defined."

> Our Party [he went on] does not agree that "the principal orientation of the anti-imperialist forces is toward the struggle against the danger of war." . . . The establishment of peace is only part of the battle against imperialism. . . . Our essential goal must be *the defeat and elimination of imperialism.* . . . We were horrified to learn that a communist leader in a capitalist country considered that the armed struggle for Latin American

independence endangered peaceful coexistence and should be proscribed by the communist movement. . . . We communists must triumph over arrogance and sectarianism. . . . The death of Che Guevara is the preamble to a new stage in the Latin American revolutionary process.

Though Rodriguez ended "by saluting the support Cuba received from the Soviet Union, the socialist camp, and the revolutionary movement," he did not hesitate to point out "the inevitable disagreements, often serious ones, in the development of friendship and collaboration with the Soviet Union." Cuba's position is therefore not unconditional adherence, like that of those countries which joined their armies to the Soviet Union's to invade Czechoslovakia.

6. Privileges and the new bureaucrats

In Cuba, as in other communist countries, the development of a group of devoted militants – whom we willingly salute even if we do not share all their ideas – has been paralleled by that of a group of careerists and social climbers. A group of men whom the people call "belly communists" – men looking for jobs that will enable them to eat well – has appeared on the scene. To *socialismo* they oppose *socialismo*, which can be defined as a buddy system. The man in a position to provide certain products or favors willingly grants them to his friends and relations – expecting similar services from them when the chance comes.

The delegation of power to those whom Castro trusts is rather feudal in nature. The Party is still suffused with that Spanish-American mentality which willingly conceded all powers to the leader, the *caudillo*. Castro, *le grand seigneur*, lives very comfortably; he understands that his aides have extensive needs, and he sometimes recompenses them in a lordly fashion. His faithful were recently given free Alfa Romeos: a modern conception of the feudal grant, or a sort of socialist plus-value. In July 1969 it was said that there were six hundred of these cars in Cuba and that the man who drew up the lists of recipients would be in a position to know who *really* held the reins of power that year. If the rector of the University of Havana still goes to work in a Soviet jeep it's only because he is not eager to have the students see his handsome Alfa Romeo. Since power is delegated from above it seems normal, in Cuba, to compensate those with responsibilities. The simplicity of life in North

Vietnam, where cadres and even top leaders live in austerity, would be unimaginable in Havana, where officials rejected in horror an advantageous motorbicycle deal that would have permitted enormous economies in foreign exchange and fuel.

But it is not just a matter of cars. There are also the beautiful villas and the magnificent Varadero beach where officers and their families vacation free of charge. I had previously been impressed by the contrast between the simple lives of the Cuban ministers and the ill-considered spending of their African counterparts. But this comparison can no longer be made without certain reservations. I understand more fully Castro's angry reaction to my protests on the lavishness of a banquet given for me at Victorino. He had felt the indirect personal reproach, and he was not mistaken. When I had similarly protested against an overlavish reception in Hanoi in March 1964 Prime Minister Phan Van Dong's response had been quite different: "I see your point."

To all this must be added the sexual privileges of "the new class," and these are important in Cuba. The important official who happens to be married can use the excuse of night-time meetings or meetings in the country to see his girlfriend or friends. But in the barracks of the *macheteros* who cut the cane there are sometimes little signs that read, "Sleep quietly, the revolution is watching over your wife." As a matter of fact, if a *machetero*'s wife is visited by a man, her husband may get a telegram about it from the local CDR. Sexual privileges are thus reserved to the rich and to the imported foreign experts, eagerly sought out by young Cuban women. These privileges are more marked for men – Che Guevara dismissed a young woman in charge of a government bureau because her husband would not allow her to travel without him. Mao Tsetung reminds us that there is no true revolution without the liberation of women. But *machismo*, male privilege, is far from abolished in Cuban society.

And so a new ruling caste is being established in Cuba. It is certainly well-disposed toward the workers and the poor, but often in a paternalistic way. Solidly established in its privileges, suffering no privation, this new class does not really understand the people's material difficulties and is insufficiently concerned with improving them. One senses the possibility of a leftist opposition that could make the idealist Che Guevara its standard bearer: as it is now some are content with covert opposition, others would like to emigrate. (I disapprove of this latter position, since it seems a policy of despair, but it is easier to say this from Paris than in Havana.)

Cuban socialism, like its Soviet model, honors the family and conjugal virtues, and urges illegitimate couples to marry – in other words, it has a traditional morality. But by reducing (as a step toward eliminating) material incentives in the Cuban economy, it refuses a man the opportunity to work *first* for his family, his wife, his children, his parents. This preferential love need not exclude devotion to the nation, the collectivity, the revolution. A man can be a good communist and still be more concerned with the health of his children, the fatigue of his wife, than with that of other people. But even today it requires a fair amount of money to alleviate these basic problems in Cuba. The only other solution is to try to live in a monastic atmosphere – something the Russians are tending to renounce and that even the Chinese do not advocate.

The economic results of this refusal are already evident in Cuban life and the inadequate amount of work furnished by the masses is an immediate consequence. It therefore cannot be justified economically. Rodriguez has willingly admitted that production would increase more rapidly if material incentives were used. But, he said, "if it were to become the most important element, it would lead us from socialism, as we have seen happen in Yugoslavia and Czechoslovakia." We can see the link between this rejection of material incentive and a political conception opposed to all liberalization!

Back in 1960 I warned Castro of the danger of choosing state enterprises to the exclusion of cooperative formulas. In the Soviet Union a large-scale attempt to expand state farms at the expense of the kolkhozes was suddenly halted in 1961 in the face of the general economic inferiority of the sovkhozes. Only the Yugoslav *combinat* provides better results – and this was especially true after self-management had been introduced.

Rodriguez told me that a state-controlled economy could function better if the workers had wider latitude in expressing their opinions. (Yet at the Moron refinery, which was having a great deal of trouble with its water-cooling machinery, a worker described how the problem had been simply solved in "former days," and the *companeros* waxed indignant because he hadn't suggested this solution earlier. "But it's been eight or nine years since we workers were asked for our opinions on production!" In some ways the

5

workers are as despised as ever.) Rodriguez also admitted that a
"combination of self-management at the group level and material
incentives at the enterprise level would be efficacious. But this could
lead," he went on, "to certain grave distortions in the national
economy." He wanted an economic structure in which democratic
participation by consumers would allow for expression of their
wants within the framework of a state-controlled economy. But
this would require that the structure and mentality of Cuba's
politico-military orientation be completely modified. In late 1969,
writing in *Le Monde*, the economists Ota Sik and Jacqueline Vernes
showed that this could be done if an economy used its planning for
general concepts, for the satisfaction of basic and collective needs,
but permitted the free working of the market to facilitate expression
of demand.

Similarly a Cuban worker should feel more directly and personally
linked to the production process than he does today. In some
quarters an attempt is being made to achieve this by political and
moral means, but to be honest such means have never functioned
well. The current militarization in Cuba is abandoning the workers
and turning its back on socialism. Given the present state of our
knowledge, to deny material incentives and the advantages of a
partially free market is to deny their political corollary: a certain
liberalization. This seriously threatens to impede future Cuban
progress; it does so at the expense of the poor, the least provided
for, those to whom a true socialism would give priority since its
purpose is to reduce social injustices.

7. Protosocialism with a military bureaucracy

One French writer has called the Russian and Chinese systems (thus
considering them more or less alike) "protosocialisms with national
bureaucracies." I would use a similar expression in regard to Cuba.
Certain elements of socialism are to be found in Cuba, but turning
over to the state the ownership of the means of production, distribution, and information doesn't necessarily lead to their socialization.
What it really does is place them at the disposition of a directive
group – in the final analysis, that of Fidel Castro.

This does not mean that the worker is master of his tools, or that
the peasant is master of his land and livestock; the latter has actually
been, or is in the process of being, dispossessed of them. It does not
mean that demand regulates the orientation of production, for there

has been an arbitrary decision – which can legitimately be seen as excessive, even if essential – to grant priority to exports. What it does mean is that there are certain bases on which one day might be built what I call socialism. The first thing about socialism is that it calls for the reduction of social injustices and the *real participation* of all workers in basic decisions and major policy orientations. This socialism is based not only on the collective ownership of property, but on the truly *democratic management* of the means of production, which thus protects the general interest.

To begin with socialism implies the rejection of censorship, which, according to a 1968 manifesto of Czech intellectuals "has put us back a hundred years. Censorship prevents the exchange of information and opinions, it makes an informed public opinion impossible, it favors the publication of foolishness, it makes power more difficult to control, it protects incompetent officials, and it permits other immoralities. It makes art and science mere servants of power, ornaments tolerated on the façade of the state."

The socialist regime is voluntarist, and it can therefore make many errors, often without knowing how to correct them quickly enough. Only unhampered criticism can hasten the acquisition of the knowledge indispensable to increased efficiency. Socialism should allow for the blossoming of all individuals who accept the priority of collective tasks – once these tasks really become *theirs* because they participated in the decision. But the time has come to try to draw some conclusions and present them with the modesty that Castro judiciously urges on all technicians and scientists. (He would be well advised to listen to his own counsel of modesty, and it is the duty of his real friends to remind him of this.)

Writing about Nasser, Bourguiba, Sihanouk and Nkrumah (who in many ways remind one of Castro), Jean Lacouture concluded: "Their methods can be traced back to a romantic paternalism that is neither a good developer of conscience, nor a good executor of responsibilities, nor proper to the institutionalization of authority."* We are of course speaking here of Latin America, where the weighty presence of North American imperialism often operates through abominable dictators in Brazil, Argentina, Paraguay, the Dominican Republic, Nicaragua, and Guatemala, to say nothing of the gangsters

* *Quatre hommes et leur peuples, surpouvoir et sous-développement*, Le Seuil, 1969.

in Haiti and elsewhere. True, Castro has inherited a difficult sociological situation: two almost incompatible civilizations, the one rural and the other urban. A Caribbean revolution cannot result in European democracy. But one must continue in one's constructive criticism of *all* established governments.

8

"Revolution is not easy, you know!"

1. What is to be done?

"Revolution is not easy, you know." This acknowledgement by Castro shows that he is eager to do better, and this is to his credit. The criticisms in this book should not make us forget that we are dealing with a man of good will, eager to improve his people's lot. He is always trying to learn, always striving, but the prolonged exercise of power has convinced him that he understands every problem better than anybody else, which is obviously impossible. However, far be it from me to compare Castro, as some Yankees do, with the Latin American dictators that they themselves support!

Nobody knows if Cuba will one day achieve a certain kind of communism or, if this should happen, what kind of communism it would be. If Cuba does not achieve communism this wouldn't necessarily mean a return to capitalism, for there are many ways to improve and extend the various types of socialism, or non-capitalist development, through which Cuba could pass. There is no great risk in stating that Cuba's eventual communism, something not very likely to come about, would be very different, or even totally distinct, from the outlines imprudently sketched by Castro.

Future societies will be considerably more dynamic, will change more rapidly than their present promoters predict. They will be full of contradictions and, as time goes by, will take on forms that we cannot even begin to imagine. I can foresee the possibility that changes wrought in genetics will one day play a part in the personality of the man of tomorrow, and thus in society. They will not necessarily be beneficial changes; we already know the destructive possibilities of atomic energy. It is best not to speculate, lest we too fall into imprudent prophesying.

Let us concern ourselves with more immediate realities. The short- and medium-term future of Cuban socialism during the next fifteen or twenty years is likely – while other Cuban government officials fear to oppose Castro's absolute power – to remain over-dependent on the man who is today seldom called the *líder maximo* – as he often was in 1963 – but is rather generally referred to as the commander-in-chief, the Prime Minister, and, more rarely, the First Secretary of the Party. "Commander-in-chief" is a title that immediately puts us in the military context, that of obedience "without hesitation or complaint," that which no longer permits real possibilities of discussion. The most striking aspect of the situation is to see Castro surrounded by people who almost never contradict him; this makes him a *man alone*.

A man alone – or rather a man who has progressively isolated himself and no longer feels at ease except with his old comrades from the Sierra or with anonymous workers. Napoleon's triumph was due to his team of marshals, which he was careful not to decimate. But how many ministers and high government and Party officials in Cuba have been dismissed, removed from power and responsibili-ties, in recent years? I dare not name, lest I do them harm, all those officials whom I met in 1960 and 1963 who have now been relegated to minor posts, or who have left or are planning to leave Cuba.

The man who wants to keep his job had better not contradict Castro. And because this is well understood he is surrounded by an atmosphere of fear, if not of obsequiousness and sometimes even of denunciation. Men who have managed to get jobs for which they are not really qualified are often inclined to use dubious means to protect them. We have already seen how Castro sometimes makes hasty decisions without adequate research, instead of giving serious attention to specialists and then either deciding for the majority or for those who seem most competent.

Having begun by prematurely outlining a radiant future, he is now forced to make promises that are more and more grandiloquent, but less and less convincing. His people are waiting to see what will happen. If his promises of abundance completely fall through there is the risk of a kind of general cold war between the masses of non-militant workers and the authorities; some aspects of this are already apparent.

The enormous mass of Cuba's agricultural investments – irriga-tion works, heavy equipment, roads, plantations, fertilizers, herbi-cides, and pesticides – will bring a mediocre return if the situation develops as the struggle did in Russia between the peasants and the authorities in 1929–33, and if the "don't-give-a-damn" attitude becomes widespread. Efficiency has never been outstanding, but it could diminish even further. For the grandiose plans to be realized, it is necessary that everybody on the job do his best, be animated by a real revolutionary awareness. The awareness limited to official posters and speeches of Party officials threatens to lead to an increasingly police-oriented state.

It should be pointed out that what follows are my *opinions*, offered without inhibition since I was asked for them, and not my *advice*. Since only one-fifth of Cuba's traditional agricultural workers have remained in the fields, the agricultural labor contributed by the urban mobilizations is no longer simply the added extra it was at the beginning; it has become the basic supply of available labor. It is therefore urgent that these mobilizations be made more efficient. The first thing to be done is to eliminate night work, except for heavy equipment or during peak periods. The next thing to be done is to mobilize volunteers only for every other Sunday, but this time for real work, for an intense effort related to defined norms, achieved by working in the fields from seven in the morning to noon. However, the long-term mobilizations will continue to be the most efficient, and it is on these that the greatest emphasis must be placed.

As long ago as 1960 I recommended that it would be best to put Cuba's city dwellers in a situation where they could work well with a minimum of effort – using light, modern hand-tools such as are used in European gardens. The most important thing is to achieve a more efficient organization of the work, and this would begin to improve if, as in China, workers were more often called on for their advice. Better organized mobilizations, led by older technicians who have returned to work as well as by the young people now coming en masse from the institutes, would quickly create a more productive atmosphere. This would incite the mobilized workers to make a greater effort. It's not very encouraging to hoe coffee plants when you've just finished pulling others up from nearby fields.

Given the scale of the big plans, the slightest overall error becomes very costly. Hiring foreign specialists on cane, fodder, citrus fruits, coffee, bananas, agricultural procedures and experimentation would be much more profitable and considerably cheaper than buying hundreds of bulldozers, caterpillars, and tractors which are only necessary because of the poor utilization and maintenance of Cuba's agricultural equipment.

In terms of Cuba's present stage of political development and attitudes the most serious errors cannot be eliminated if material incentives are reduced to their present level. We should not prematurely concentrate on communism in the twenty-first century, but let each generation resolve its own problems. It is more urgent to consider the immediate future of Latin American revolutionary movements whose eyes are turned toward Cuba – even if only to criticize it.

If the tractor teams were to receive the base salary of agricultural workers (a salary already doubled, in this hypothesis) plus significant bonuses corresponding to the quality and quantity of work furnished, they would take greater care of their machines, they would be more concerned to find replacements for broken parts, and they would try to use their equipment better. . . . These bonuses would be more attractive if they were paid in goods, in an improvement of board, or in clothes. Each permanent team could be given the means of voluntarily producing on its own a part of its food supply, those products easiest to grow on a small scale. (I suggested this in my 1960 reports.) A Chinese-style work check wouldn't involve too much bureaucracy.

A simplification of the administrative organism and a generalization of vertical integrations would permit production to be controlled by factories or organs of distribution. In addition to the fish and tobacco boards (the latter have gone a bit too far), there could be similar organizations for vegetables, rice, coffee, citrus fruits, tubers and bananas, milk, meats, etc. It seems excessive to say that the future political evolution of Cuba would be compromised by these suggested measures. Its future is considerably more threatened by militarization, and especially by the absence of freedom of the press and free expression.

Material interest should not be the only stake. To despise the Cuban worker by believing him attached *only* to his wages would be to go to the other extreme – as Castro justly points out, it would not have been worth making a revolution. But as an additional way to arouse his interest, the most valuable moral incentive would be respect for his individuality *as a worker*. That implies discussion open to all: not only as concerns production plans and policy but also as to the daily organization of work, about which each man often has something very useful to say.

As in China, time would certainly be lost in such discussion, but there would also be valuable improvements. In addition, it would contribute to the absolutely irreplaceable feeling on the part of the worker that he is really *participating* in the management of his enterprise, that he *personally* contributes to decisions about the nature and the quality of his work. He would see that this work is not decided on only in high places, as was done under the capitalist owner. The application of such a principle would result in more initiative, more responsibility, and more autonomy for *small* work units.

Let us re-examine the Oriente rice plan, with 65,000 hectares of rice fields in 1970. The *ganadero* promoted to supervisor was not competent to discuss the general strategy of an operation of such dimensions. But this plan is divided into districts somewhat on the scale of the former *granjas* with 3000 to 5000 hectares each. If these districts were given a real personality, with a certain amount of self-management and financial responsibility, some permanent workers, and a fixed grant of day-to-day material, then each worker could efficiently participate in its management, finally feel at home, and understand that his work and his comrades' work would result in direct and personal profit. Such a structure would facilitate the organization of work and enable present officials to cope with it.

As to capital investment priorities – at present determined mainly by physical criteria – they do not sufficiently take into account the speed with which a given expense will lead to productive returns. Credits are made available to plans mainly in terms of material, equipment and fertilizer, for example, without a reliable index of comparative returns. Money credits are supplied only to meet salaries. In all cases the grants are budgetary, not loans that have to be repaid. The plan is therefore not particularly concerned with the economic efficiency of these grants.

The notion of interest on money no longer applies, and all receipts are paid into the budget. Nobody in these enterprises is concerned for them to be profitable, and not all are equally motivated by a sense of doing their duty. It would seem that Cuba is determined to repeat the series of economic improvisations that one after the other have already been recognized as dangerous by other socialist states.

The leaders in the renaissance of socialist economic thought – the Russians Trapeznikov, Nemtchinov, Novojilov; the Poles Lange and Brus; the Czechs Sik, Kouba, Levcik; the Hungarian Bognar, and many others – all affirm that the overall objectives of a central development plan should largely be set in operation by the mechanism of automatic reactions to incitations; in short, by the market mechanisms. This in no way implies that the means of production cease to be collective – on the contrary. To be effective, the plan needs the market.

Sik in particular has noted the important characteristics that distinguish this organized system from a capitalist market. In a socialist economy, the market's principal role is as an indicator. But though it supplies information about the usefulness of past and future products, it cannot in itself determine the future development of production. There is thus no possibility of a return to a spontaneity that does not correspond to the optimum development of productive structures. Nor is it the market that supplies information on desirable collective consumption and on the overall structure of revenues. All these choices are made by the planning center, which represents the nation's collective interest.*

The interest paid on a loan represents a delay in the attainment of wealth, a delay that has a real economic value and on which penalties should be imposed if one is aiming for maximum investment efficiency. Its absence in Cuba is allied to a certain negligence of the people's present needs. Instead of correcting the defective functioning of the small horticultural *granjas* the Cubans have replaced them with giant plans that function no better and in which the errors to be avoided may well be multiplied on a larger scale.

Here, as in Russia in about 1960, the imbalance of prices is a basic obstacle. According even to Cuban officials, prices are arbitrary and artificial. This should have prompted efforts to establish better price scales, better relations between the monetary mass and the value of available goods, rather than a desire progressively to eliminate market relations. This latter tendency led to the third agrarian reform – which expropriated the peasants as a logical follow-up to the March 13, 1968 revolutionary offensive. The peasants reacted quickly to the errors made by ACOPIO (the state purchasing organism) in establishing price relations by emphasizing overpaid productions at the expense of others, which were generally the essential ones.

If financial control were added to the parameters of physical efficacy – pretty much the only ones used to date – it would be possible to establish a better order of priorities, and thus more efficient

* Jacqueline Vernes, "Planning and the Market in Socialist Countries," *Le Monde*, September 23, 1969.

investments. If true agricultural operations of reasonable dimensions were re-created, it would be easier to establish responsibilities and penalties on an individual basis. Under the present structure these responsibilities are watered down on all sides, and the choice of leaders is over-dependent on Castro's moods and chance meetings. It is therefore not made on a rational basis.

A Romanian friend whom I met on my return from Cuba told me he felt that the essential cause of the relative economic back-wardness of his country was the impossibility of saying what one thinks. Cadres are selected very much as a result of friendships, as well as on the basis of their political reputation. He added that though friendship often plays an important role in launching a career in a capitalist country also, there the man who has been given a "boost" has to show proof of real ability if he is to continue his upward climb. This was less true, he thought, in an authoritarian socialist regime. The key word here is "authoritarian". This brings us back to political considerations; as Mao Tse-tung points out, "politics are at the command post."

2. Political participation: the end of democratic centralism?

For many years Stalin had uncontrolled power not only over his own country but – looking back it now seems incredible – over communists everywhere in the world. This Soviet domination could not continue indefinitely, especially after China, a much more populous country than Russia, became communist – even though at first China made declarations of strict obedience. The Moscow Congress of Communist and Workers' Parties in 1969 was an attempt to tighten the reins, to reaffirm Soviet hegemony, to try to obtain the condemnation of the Chinese "heretics". But it nevertheless admitted, at least in principle, that each communist party had the right to define its own political orientation. Polycentrism is therefore accepted (except when it applies to the strategic area of the east European popular democracies, which are a part of the private domain of Soviet neocolonialism).

The end of Cominterns and Cominforms – therefore of so-called democratic centralism on an international level – should logically have led to the end of democratic centralism within each communist party. The Italian party seems close to admitting this, but the French party unhesitatingly continues to excommunicate all those who refuse to bend to its will.

The necessity for discipline under socialism is understandable, especially when a country must emerge rapidly from underdevelopment. But as we have shown, precipitation should not be mistaken for speed. As for Cuba, such discipline is in no way incompatible with the participation of all in decision-making, especially if we bear in mind Fidel Castro's extraordinary powers of persuasion – of which he might make better use. This would presuppose democratic discussions within the party cells and other party divisions, and then within production units. Without in any way negating socialism, there could be general participation in local, regional, and provincial power, as well as in the management of social services, etc.

Participation in Cuba today is limited, and it may not impinge on the domain reserved to Castro. But that domain would profit by being limited to essential points: defense and security. Socialism demands true popular participation at all levels of decision-making. In Cuba, the present Party mechanisms provide for nothing more than a means of registering approval of government policy. Almost nobody tries to find out what the workers, the cadres, the intellectuals, and the peasants think. It is unlikely that the latter would have approved their dispossession. Cuba should try to free itself of this personal power for, although it may initially have been partly justified by the general underdevelopment, it is now losing more and more of its justification as the average cultural level rises. Yet it is now trying to maintain itself, if necessary against the majority, by support from the military and bureaucratic castes, from the army and the Party. Leaders of these groups are often hard workers, but they also defend their caste privileges and, above all, their thirst for power.

Castro would not accept control from below because he has enjoyed personal power too long to be able to give it up gradually. It is therefore up to the country's other political leaders – especially Raul Castro, Dorticós, Rodriguez, Armando Hart, and Blas Roca – to advise him to do so, if they have the courage and if they realize that the present personal dictatorship power structure threatens a series of difficulties that may lead to catastrophe. Revolutionary Cuba began by attempting an unusual socialism, and the Castro of 1960 loudly disclaimed Stalinism. He does not seem to realize the extent to which he is increasingly following a not dissimilar path.

If democracy is to be brought to Cuba in progressive stages and without endangering socialism's economic conquests, the more lucid elements of the Party must understand the gravity of the situation. Opposition to political liberalization, which seems so necessary to me, will not be limited to Castro, even if he leads it. It may well stem from the ruling group as a whole, most of whom come from a bourgeoisie whose way of thinking was shaped by their Spanish-American past.

No matter what it *says*, this bourgeoisie on the whole continues to despise the people. Its concern with the people is paternalistic; it explains to the people what it *has* to do and, more seriously, what it has to think. This "communist bourgeoisie" clings to power by flattering the leader – and at the same time making sure it doesn't suffer too much from shortages. Such a view may seem too black. In any case, the reality is more complex and undoubtedly more mixed with positive features. My concern here is to highlight the dark spots to see how they can be improved. The obsequiousness of these leaders, who are not concerned, or not sufficiently concerned, with the misery of the people, led one reader of this book to a harsh judgement. Aren't we dealing here, he asked me, with a sort of "*Lumpen-bourgeoisie*" without sufficient morality to justify its powers?

Generalization always leads to exaggeration. There are pure souls in Cuba whom everyone respects. I was particularly struck to hear an old *gusano* salute the sincerity of Rodriguez. It's high time that these leaders better understood the people's needs and aspirations. This can be done if the people are allowed to express themselves freely. The present regime brings to mind a kind of "enlightened despotism". Let us not forget that despotism has always been badly enlightened, and that power corrupts.

The time has come to progress from this sort of renewed absolute monarchy to a more modern version of what I will oversimplify in calling limited, if not constitutional, monarchy. The entire population, and not only the ruling group and those most submissive to its will, could then participate in power. The present problem is that those who could be helpful, who want to serve but are not completely convinced, have been shoved aside and feel excluded from their community. It is as if they had been excommunicated. It would seem possible to reintegrate many of these people, instead of continuing to force them to leave. If all noncomformists were to leave Cuba, the result would be an irreparable human loss.

3. The Cuban agronomy

In 1959–60 China's food problems were infinitely more severe than Cuba's. In the hectic year of 1958 China also tried to progress to communism too quickly with the Great Leap Forward and the people's communes. In 1960 it was hard-hit by the withdrawal of Soviet aid, plans, and technicians. But during this same time it continued to pay off its debts to Russia and never cut off its aid to Cambodia, Indonesia, parts of Africa, and even Cuba. And it accelerated a strong effort to develop nuclear weapons, all this while suffering from fearful weather conditions that seriously harmed the agricultural base of its economy.

Cuba never suffered from a food shortage as severe as that in China in 1959–61, when in certain times and regions the word "famine" could have been applied. And China never had so developed an infrastructure as Cuba's, or similar import resources, or comparable quantities of fertilizer and equipment. And yet by 1962 China was emerging from its food difficulties. True, China has a more courageous peasantry, but it also has a government that knows how to correct its errors more speedily.*

Given its fertile land, its level of technique, its tractors, and its fertilizers – all infinitely superior to the resources at China's disposal – there is no reason for Cuba's failure to end the shortage of fruit and vegetables that has been going on since 1961. Castro's praise of the sacrifices of the pyramid builders would be tolerable only if he shared in these sacrifices. Neglect of the people's need for food amounts to contempt; a better-led, better-equipped and better-aided peasantry could easily have met these needs while the state farms saw to export requirements. Not to have done this was political dogmatism. I must say so again, even at the risk of displeasing: my object is not to please Castro but to help Cuba and the revolutions that are to come.

The sacrifice of food crops and the assignment of first priority to export products is the most serious charge that must be brought against the oligarchies of the Third World. It is even an essential

* In the correction of these errors, what was the role of Liu Shao-chi, now condemned by the country's leaders? It is difficult to specify precisely, but nevertheless treachery corresponds to excessive schematization. It would have been nice to have heard his version of events. . . . As long as there is a monopoly on information the official version is suspect. It is said that Liu had been a traitor since at least 1949. Why then was he allowed to continue?

characteristic of underdevelopment, for it allows developed econo-mies to wring large profits from the backward countries. The world sugar market is so glutted that exporting countries become depen-dent on those that "charitably" buy this surplus product. The Chinese made this plain to the Cubans in 1965–6. In October 1968 Cuba signed the international sugar agreement that gave it a 2·1 million ton export quota on the western market. But this agreement was rejected by the United States, the principal importer. Nor was it accepted by the European Economic Community, which wanted a 1·2 million ton export quota, even though it was paying the wildly excessive price of $17 a ton for beet sugar. Thus the European tax payer is invited to finance an extravagant sugar dumping at a time when sugarcane is a better producer than sugar beet, and *we pretend to help developing nations*. (This hypocrisy demonstrates, if we need such demonstration, the power of the European sugar beet lobby.)

Castro reasons politically, sentimentally, passionately, and tech-nically rather than economically. He thinks that a perfect ultra-modern technique can by itself solve his overall economic problems. The first thing he said to me in our June 1969 meeting was: "Talk to me about techniques, but not about economics." I was bowled over by the lack of understanding that this revealed. As though one could resolve the complex problems of development by simply choosing the best technique – without taking into account the restraints and limitations imposed by the economy. His decision to give sugar priority, abandoned in 1959–60 and then re-established after 1963, had, as we have seen, some justification, but it was pushed too far. And it became one of the principal causes – along with the disorganization of state enterprises and the rejection of cooperatives – of the prolongation of Cuba's food problem. The west European market – assuming the economically unfavorable prospect of a continued break between Cuba and the United States – could by 1980 absorb at least 200,000 tons of Cuban early winter vegetables and fruit annually, as well as considerably greater quan-tities of beef, if they could be furnished. Cuba would then be able to obtain from that part of Europe all the equipment it cannot get – at least in modern models – in the socialist countries.

At that point Cuba would no longer be so dependent on the Soviet economy, and it could reaffirm its political independence, achieving a certain neutrality in the socialist camp. If it wanted to it could then follow the "Vietnamese" line and try to maintain a position more equally balanced between China and Russia. True, Soviet dependence is less of a burden for the distant Cubans than the Yankee yoke, but more independence would be pleasant. May not a better understanding between the United States and Russia one day cause Russia to further reduce its aid to Cuba? This hypothesis cannot be rejected out of hand.

4. The "holy terror" and the flatterers

Fidel Castro is an historical figure, an exceptional being, who gave his revolution and his country an extraordinary position out of proportion to Cuba's geographical importance. Until now, two opinions about him have been chiefly current. For the Americans and their allies, for the world that somewhat too hastily calls itself free, but which I shall call rich, and which its enemies somewhat schematically call imperialistic, Castro is a dangerous enemy, a dictator. For Cuba's unconditional supporters, especially those not in Cuba, the dominant feeling is one of admiration, to the point where all critical objectivity is lost. This is scarcely possible for Cubans. For the rest of us, neither of these extreme positions is satisfactory. Castro has certainly never been afraid to risk his life for his ideals, and this always merits respect. Yet by 1972 he had been in a position of more or less unlimited power for thirteen years – a factor that cannot help but endanger the quality of some of his arguments.

In the midst of severe shortages foreign progressives are received with excessive luxury. Very few of them demand to share even a part of the general austerity. Though their reception demonstrates an honorable sense of hospitality on the part of the Cuban leaders, it is not the latter who suffer from privations. Sociologists tell me that the pride of a traditional society is always flattered by entertaining its guests grandly; let's not forget the Spanish-grandee side of Castro. Among communist rulers the tradition is of Stalinist origin: hopefully, on the basis of what he himself receives, the visitor will get an impression of general abundance. Strangely enough, the trick has worked for decades. The unconditional progressive supporters "profit" from these pleasant free excursions that keep them in a certain euphoria. Once they get home, they naturally all become propagandists, partly from conviction but also because they're eager to be reinvited. "If you were to soften your thinking somewhat," two friends told me, "your book would be more useful."

But I would like Fidel Castro to come down from his platform (or his jeep) with a mind more open to all criticism. His responsibilities are crushing; he can no longer single-handedly carry them out correctly.

Since Khrushchev's downfall – a precedent he might well meditate on – the Soviet collegiate system has not been very efficacious. It has become clearly oriented toward neo-Stalinist conservatism, and it has actually gone from the cult of personality to the absence of personality! Cuba's direction could be as different as the historical development of the two countries has been. The individualistic tendencies of this Latinized and Americanized people are stronger than those of the descendents of the nomadic Slavs. I would never advise a return to the domination of North American trusts in conjunction with a façade of pseudo-democratic parliamentarianism, the inadequacy of which was equal to the bad taste of the buildings that symbolized it, and a return to which is in any case impossible. But there are many possibilities other than a return to the past.

The Cuba of 1959–60 was confusedly trying to establish a really unusual socialism. The Cuba of 1970–2 has after more than a decade accumulated an enormous mass of experience of the highest significance. The time has come to establish a balance sheet and try to formulate *new*, unusual solutions. A balance sheet would not be honest if it could not accept constructive criticism – whether from inside or outside the country – in attempting to draw the best possible conclusions from its analyses.

The beginnings were promising: the people joyously participating in the symbolic burial of the trusts, rushing to the Bay of Pigs, risking death for their revolution. Arts and letters were not put under Zhdanovian pressure, though there was already censorship of the press. But a bureaucratic process has since continued to develop; to some extent Castro's personality has been a force against it, since he has in some ways maintained obvious good will and a high level of morality.

These positive accomplishments were accompanied by the unfortunate number of economic failures that we have discussed; these must be recognized as such; and they are not merely the result of bad luck. Attempts must be made to arrive at a better comprehensive explanation, linked to the nature of power, to the strategy of Cuban development, and to the struggles of the various social

categories* as well as to the struggles within the ruling group –
struggles of which I was only able to get glimpses. In the shadow
of Castro, the army, and the Party, a privileged "new class" is
establishing itself. This is perhaps more serious than the commander-in-chief's personal errors. What is the ideology of this
class? It is difficult to say if it has a comprehensive ideology. I think
its ideology tends rather to be heterogeneous, except in its taste for
power and the privileges that stem from power. It considers itself
an avant-garde, but the role is self-attributed and cannot be justified
either by sufficient competence or, especially, by social consciousness.

It would be interesting to compare this group with the Chinese
avant-garde, which is closer to the masses and better understands its
ideas and needs. As my colleague at the Institut Agronomique
Chominot told me, if the avant-garde shows a superior political and
moral awareness it can move the ideas of the masses to a higher level
of comprehension and then offer them a line of conduct within their
grasp. All this would obviously necessitate greater reflection and a
better knowledge of the milieu.

I am inclined to think that dogmatism, with its corollary of unlimited personal power (which obscures judgement), is the principal
causes of Cuba's present difficulties. It was *a priori* decided to
eliminate all forms of cooperatives in agricultural production as well
as in the crafts and in distribution. (Lenin acknowledged the
socialist character of cooperatives; only Stalin placed above them
state property, incorrectly seen as belonging to "all the people.")
The elimination of market relations inhibits and even prevents
serious economic analyses. The revolutionary has been preferred to
the expert, when an attempt should have been made to retain all
Cubans with something to contribute to the revolution, even nonconformists. By giving abusive privileges to those who are (or call
themselves, for it's easy to do) revolutionaries, there is a strong risk
of corrupting them, of making them incapable of correcting the
situation. Private activity was eliminated and the peasantry definitively dispossessed before this was economically or politically
justifiable. All this has led to a hyper-stratified structure, proudly

---

* Young French sympathizers who spent a long time in Cuba reproached
me for not having made such a study, whereas they themselves had been in a
position to do it. One of them advised me to limit myself to an exposé of the
facts and avoid political interpretation. You can't please everybody. I do what
I can, and risk the chance of error.

referred to as being "the most socialized in the world" (but alas neither the most efficient nor the most democratic), of giant production units too difficult to organize, given the present skills of the technicians. And the waiting lines lengthen. The people have deserved better.

It is time for Castro to think over his responsibilities, and this will only be possible if he renounces control over details and stops making a show of himself. His extravagant promises belong more and more to the realm of fable. The difficulties have made him turn over economic powers to the army, which has accepted them joyously.

Castro adds up his tractors, his fertilizers, and his men, and deduces a given volume of production. He tries to inspire his *companeros* with his own revolutionary awareness, but fails to see that unlike him they are not sustained by the exaltation of power. He takes his *desire* for a level of consciousness to be a fact, and he builds an entire social structure predicated on this high level, which is far from being attained. And the evil results of this structure lead him to what must be recognized as a military dictatorship. Force is therefore substituted for good will.

The need for a Cuban balance sheet is made the more urgent by the fact that Latin America is at a turning point, the orientation of which could be helped by the Cuban experience. The value of this experience would quickly increase if it were learned that the waiting lines in Havana had been reduced and then eliminated; that vegetables, fruit, fish, and yogurt are on all Cuban tables; and that serious criticism can be printed in Cuban newspapers without the writer being charged with counter-revolutionary attitudes, the modern equivalent of lèse-majesté. In all sincerity it must be said that in 1971 this did not seem to be the trend. This makes me rather nervous about the future of the Cuban revolution; let us, however, avoid any kind of prophecy. I was asked what post-Castroism might be like. My answer was that if it were established in 1973-4 its form would be very different from what it would be toward the end of this century or even the beginning of the next. That's cautious enough. The important thing is a certain liberalization. But how?

9

Is Cuba Socialist?

AT THE beginning of 1972 Cuba entered its fourteenth year of revolution. Though it had a hard time confronting its powerful neighbor to the north, which was aided by local allies, spies, and mercenaries, Cuba received enormous and irreplaceable aid from the socialist camp, without which it would either have had to capitulate or to suffer terribly. It even received a certain amount of sympathy – translated into experts and credits for equipment – from several western nations such as France and England. My young radical friends tell me it's preferable for certain denunciations to be made by sympathizers. This brings us back to the serious question that gives this book its name.

In the beginning, Cuba established the most socialist regime in existence, with more popular enthusiasm and freedom of expression than anywhere else in the socialist camp. Unfortunately things have changed. True, there are still many elements in Cuba that favor the construction of socialism. Cuba has solidly established its national independence by rejecting dependence on the United States, but it is economically dependent on the Soviet Union, and while this facilitates a certain form of socialism, it keeps Cuba from envisaging any other structure – for example, Chinese ideology. The Cuban state has economic and political power, and this permits it to give priority to a number of collective needs. Some of its industrial achievements constitute marked progress – cement, electricity, sugar. Fishing is making progress, and the importance given by Castro to irrigation is essential. Stock raising, fodder crops, and planting are progressing in disorder, but they are improving. Some of the workers have maintained their enthusiasm under what are difficult circumstances.

But is this state really in the hands of the people, the workers, the oppressed? It would seem too much to say so. A ruling group has gradually established itself by the successive elimination of other groups, of other leaders. It has had at its head since 1959 the same leader, and he too is uncontested. It is here that the shoe pinches most. As I see it, a country cannot call itself socialist if there is no possibility for public protest. (This lack is to varying degrees true of all the countries that now call themselves socialist. My doubts about the socialist character of Cuba therefore extend to the entire socialist camp – which is hardly likely to please them.) ⌉

Discipline is of course necessary to ensure lasting development, which requires an expanded accumulation of capital, enormous investments. This means an austerity program which would be acceptable only if it were really generalized; otherwise let's have no more talk of the simultaneous construction of communism, if you're as pragmatic as you say.

If Castro finds it necessary to pay more to the most faithful officials – those charged with making others work – he should not forget that the humblest workers would in the present stage also be responsive to material incentives. Organized into small-work collectives, into cooperative production (agriculture, crafts, etc.) and distribution units, they would have a personal interest in seeing them prosper. One may justifiably point out that such a socialism would be very imperfect; however, it could more rapidly supply food and clothing, and that's very important. It would above all be able to accommodate criticism; the anti-bureaucratic struggle could take a form adapted to the revolutionary culture of this country.

⌈ Socialist elements strike me as being very markedly on the retreat in Cuba, especially since the military effectively took over the direction of the entire economy.⌋The structure of the giant plans does not allow for an efficient organization of work. The battalions of workers and material can assure neither the quality of work nor the full utilization of expensive equipment. The cadres are overwhelmed and not always well informed. (To cite a personal example, none of my reports has been published in Cuba, and the same is true for many reports by foreign experts. If some of the information in them had been made public, it would have been possible to avoid some gross errors.) Production has become more and more expensive, and the government is increasingly calling for more effort and sacrifices, as well as for the acceptance of increased austerity. Despite constant reorganizations, it is unable to put its economy in order.

"No democratic discussion within the Party," Cuba's highest political officials told me, though they knew my position well. It must be sadly true. The military are eliminating many of the old communists from command positions. Though I am far from approving the policies of the latter, they nevertheless often try to check some abuses. Castro, commander-in-chief of the armed revolutionary forces, has a personal power over which there is inadequate control. We have seen that this often leads to hasty improvisations, premature generalizations, dangerous haste, and characteristic economic errors.

[The rejection of serious economic analyses prevents Cuba's determination of a better order of priorities; it interferes with the most judicious assignment of an enormous mass of investments, which are thereby made less efficient. Above all it leads to a situation in which the workers become less and less enthusiastic, work less and less hard. "Why did my mother ever let me be born in this lousy country?" I heard a despairing young man shout as he left a Havana movie theater.

[Castro is aware of only some of the difficulties, because his entourage doesn't dare report them all. But he must accept a certain limitation of his powers before it's too late, based on the *effective* control of the Party by the workers, of the Central Committee by the Party, and of Castro by the Committee; it is an indispensable preamble, the essential condition for economic recovery and real Cuban independence. By giving all power to the army, a nation weakens its economy and, in the final analysis, its capacity for national defense.]

Yes, I know: this is all too easy to write at an old professor's desk, in old Europe – it is not the best environment in which to understand a young revolution. But *muchisimas gracias*, Fidel, for the opportunity for a fascinating study.

Appendix: 1972

THIS study, written in 1969–70, first appeared in France in March 1970 and was strongly criticized. I was told of a fierce refutation that Cuban officials were going to circulate widely in four languages. I would have been greatly interested in such a critique, since I knew my documentation would be considered inadequate by an historian. I was not always able to verify my data adequately, sometimes having to rely on informants. The choice of facts was arbitrary, their interpretation sometimes imprudent, if not risky, the tone too assured. A serious critique would have enabled me to improve this work, which also represented a debatable political action, for I no doubt insufficiently emphasized the positive aspects of the Cuban revolution. I thought them known well enough to my readers. At the same time I considered it dangerous to refuse to undertake constructive criticism because of the imperialist menace: an argument which in its time has favored the persistence of Stalinism, notably encouraged by the dogmatism of communists and certain French progressives.

This book, which I always considered imperfect, has nevertheless received some interesting support. Starting from a more politically oriented analysis, K. S. Karol, in *Guerrillas in Power*, reaches conclusions that are often close to my own, especially when he insists on Cuba's lack of political institutions.* But the most important confirmations come from the facts themselves, as well as from Fidel Castro.

By extending the sugarcane harvest, begun on July 14, 1969, to the beginning of August 1970, Cuba was able to produce about 8·5

* See also the studies by José Yglésias, Huberman and Sweezy, Herbert Matthews, and Guncher Frank. When I wrote my book I had not read any of them, yet I was nevertheless accused of mounting a "concerted attack" with Karol.

million tons of sugar. This is precisely the goal that from 1964 the great majority of experts and Cubans, including Guevara, had advised Castro to aim for. He has achieved it, but at a much higher cost, since in proposing *los diez milliones* he had to make enormous supplementary investments, had to ask for sometimes superhuman efforts. The clean and dry paddy yields of the winter harvest 1969–70 did not surpass twenty-five quintals a hectare because of faulty, late, and weed-infested plantings – and this with the new Philippine rices that can easily return twice as much. What was gained in more extensive planting was lost in lower yields, and basic costs were higher. Although the monthly rice ration has been raised to six pounds, the possibility of exporting rice, announced in 1968–9 for 1971, is fading.

I have emphasized Castro's imprudence in promising in 1968 to quadruple Cuba's milk production in two years. In a major speech on July 26, 1970 he admitted to having been very wrong. "The amount of milk collected from January to May 1970 totals 71·3 million liters, twenty-five per cent less than for the same period in 1969." I had, of course, foreseen a more modest increase than that promised by Castro, but not a decline! He continued: "In 1968 deliveries of beef amounted to 154,000 tons, 145,000 tons are foreseen for 1970. . . . We are far from being fully satisfied with the rice plans. . . . Though it is increasing, the effort that has been made for sowing pasturage is insufficient. A considerable improvement in technique is called for. . . . Failing that, we may end with a decline in livestock."

The time of careless promises is therefore over – at least for the moment – because Castro has announced that "for the 1970–75 period the situation will be even more difficult." After having enumerated numerous deficiencies, with great courage he went on to say: "I want to speak of a factor that is far from being negligible, of our own incapacity in the overall work of the revolution. . . . Our responsibility in these problems must be noted, especially *mine*. . . . Our apprenticeship as directors of that revolution has been too costly."

Castro's first admissions of weakness dated from May 20, 1970 when he announced the failure of the "great *zafra* of ten million," specifying that "the battle for the ten million was not lost by the people: we, the administrative apparatus, the directors of the revolution, were the ones to lose it. . . . Our ignorance of the problems posed by the sugar centrals prevented us from remedying various kinds of difficulties in time."]Yet the May 20 and July 26 speeches seemed at first to increase the popularity of Castro, who wanted to "turn defeat into victory." Nevertheless, nothing followed but a rather indefinite promise of democratization.["If it is not made *for* the masses, socialism fails. Deprived of the participation of the masses, socialism loses the battle, becomes bureaucratized, uses capitalist methods, retreats ideologically," said Castro. But he still made no mention of socialism *by* the masses.]Many, however, still preferred to rely on Castro himself. He disappointed them when the principal theme of his speeches for a while continued to be the struggle against absenteeism; this seemed to emphasize an orientation that was still authoritarian.

And in truth absenteeism still plagues the regime enormously: many of those who have earned enough money to buy their rations do not come to work. Many of those who do show up, come merely to get their meals and clothing allowances and work very little. Production may decrease by sixty per cent when twenty per cent of the workers in a shoe factory are absent and their production-line posts are taken over more or less inefficiently by co-workers. And the true militants, the dedicated ones who do what they can and even more, are becoming aware of the futility of their increasingly large sacrifices and the fact that the others don't give a damn; as a result, they in turn have begun to protest. This is especially true as there is no more talk of agriculture or of peasants but of workers; this would seem to foreshadow many privations.

Since Castro's prestige appears to have become seriously tarnished, oral criticism of Cuba's leadership is becoming widespread, and there is no hesitation about voicing it in public. Thieves are scarcely ever denounced, and a shoe-factory worker is no longer afraid to sell the fruit of her larceny from door to door; she would never have dared to do this before 1970. Now it's every man for himself.

In the meantime, although officials are beginning to understand the seriousness of technical problems, they still do not submit their plans to the peasants and agricultural workers, even though the latter could avoid the crude errors of certain technicians who are too imbued with theoretical science and too lacking in practical experience. In point of fact it is the petty bourgeois who seem to hold essential practical power in Cuba – they, and not the workers and peasants, who are still despised or at best condescended to by too many of these petty bourgeois political parvenus.

If this book and other criticisms have contributed even to the smallest extent to bring about any self-criticism on the part of Castro, then that would be enough to justify them in spite of their short-comings. I was impelled to write it by Fidel Castro's invitation (an invitation that I had not at all solicited), and my previous writings should have led Castro to expect criticism. I undoubtedly went further than he thought I would by also studying economic and even political problems – a private preserve – when all he asked for was technical advice.

It is absolutely indispensable to try to give all friends of the Cuban revolution a more complete and different view from that of its officials and propagandists. If future South American revolutions want to survive – without the hope of receiving from the socialist camp per capita aid comparable to that received by Cuba – they must avoid improvisations, they will have to understand better the reasons for Cuba's problems. This, then, was my ambition: as Gramsci tells us, "seek the truth, and tell it, because only the truth is revolutionary." Though this awesome truth is difficult to arrive at, we must not give up striving for it, even under the pretext of other duties and other responsibilities. This in any case should be the rule of those who call themselves scientific, but who also strive for the least injustice and the possibility for *all* to develop.

Index